CREATE THE STYLE YOU CRAVE ON A BUDGET YOU CAN AFFORD

THE SWEET SPOT GUIDE TO HOME DECOR

desha peacock

Skyhorse Publishing

Skyhorse Publishing books may be purchased in bulk at special discounts for sales promotion, corporate gifts, fund-raising, or educational purposes. Special editions can also be created to specifications. For details, contact the Special Sales Department, Skyhorse Publishing, 307 West 36th Street, 11th Floor, New York, NY 10018 or info@skyhorsepublishing.com.

Skyhorse® and Skyhorse Publishing® are registered trademarks of Skyhorse Publishing, Inc.®, a Delaware corporation.

Visit our website at www.skyhorsepublishing.com.

10 9 8 7 6 5 4 3 2 1

Library of Congress Cataloging-in-Publication Data is available on file.

ISBN: 978-1-62873-622-9

Printed in China

preface

> "WE ALL HAVE A STORY TO TELL, AND PART OF THE
> WAY WE DO THIS IS THROUGH OUR HOMES."
> INTERVIEW WITH AMERICA'S FAMOUS
> DESIGNER NATE BERKUS, *ELLE DÉCOR*

Beyond Home Décor

Create the Style You Crave on a Budget You Can Afford is different from most decorating books. It goes beyond home décor, beyond the material, and is the first book of its kind that incorporates New Thought Philosophy/Personal Development with home décor.

While filled with visual eye candy, it also explores how creatively expressing yourself in your home and gardens helps you create the life you really want to live. As the ever so popular "Law of Attraction" is causing a paradigm shift in thought, it's essential that your life, wardrobe, career, and yes, your home décor reflect the essence of who you are and your inner heart's desire. In this book, you will learn how to surround yourself with beauty and create an environment that reflects who you are and what you want so you can draw more of that into your life.

Your Style, Your Budget

Do you desire a comfy cozy home with quilts and china teacups or maybe a bit of glam to invoke your inner pop star? Are you attracted to clean modern lines or do you want to surround yourself with culturally diverse motifs to remind you of world travels and nostalgia? Perhaps it's a mix of several styles. Whatever it is, this book will help you create the style you crave on a budget you can afford.

Inspiration

In these pages you'll be inspired by stories of everyday men and women with busy lives and limited budgets who have infused personal values, meaning, and style into their homes. Instead of feeling overwhelmed, you will feel inspired as you see how others like you have done it.

Additionally, you'll discover how I created my favorite room on the tiniest of shoestrings. It's my own private Sweet Spot where I look over my garden, have a glass of wine, and work on the creative projects that give me so much joy. I call it my cabin.

Finally, you'll find tons of resources to inspire you both online and off. We'll pull it all together in a mood board and leave you inspired to create your own amazing Sweet Spot home.

I'm so glad you are here; let's begin!

Remember, your home doesn't need to be perfect, but it does need to be you!

contents

introduction

Can I share a little secret with you?

My mother and I used to drive around the historic neighborhoods of Little Rock, Arkansas, where I grew up. We would admire the tree-lined streets, unique architecture, and charming neighborhoods. Then we would drive home to our little duplex on Laramie Cove where I spent my first twelve years of life.

Those drives were full of hope and yearning—not just for a prettier home but also for a better life. And while there wasn't much I could do about it as a child, a deep desire was planted in me that one day I might live in lovely home and share it with my daughter.

I was motivated by desire, by that deep craving. That's how I was able to create it for myself. It's easy to fall into despair when you don't have the home (or life) you desire, but the secret is this: you don't have to wait to live in the style you crave; you can begin to create it now.

LET YOUR CRAVING FUEL YOU.

I'd like to encourage you to live your life in a meaningful way in all aspects of your life, and that includes being surrounded by beauty (your kind of beauty) in your home.

Rebekah's brown paper trash bag painting is mounted on simple cardboard in my foyer. This is one of my favorite places to write and have a cup of tea.

chapter 1

WHAT IS THE SWEET SPOT?

"SOME PEOPLE LOOK FOR A BEAUTIFUL PLACE,
OTHERS MAKE A PLACE BEAUTIFUL."
HAZRAT INAYAT KHAN, FOUNDER OF
UNIVERSAL SUFISM

As someone deeply passionate about connecting to a higher purpose while enjoying the present moment, I've been a student of Sweet Spot Living for over ten years now and have incorporated the concept into every part of my life—from my livelihood/career to my family and to my *home*. I began to interview people who are living in their Sweet Spot and documented their stories on *The Desha Show*, a local TV show that I produce here in Southern Vermont.

What I learned from that experience is that everyone has his/her own definition of what the Sweet Spot is. It's self-defined, meaning you get to decide what makes your life, career, or home feel good to you. Too often we are pressured by family and society to live a certain way, but there is a paradigm shift that teaches us that it's okay to allow our inner hearts and spirits to guide us and to give us faith that we are on the right path.

When it comes to the home, it's very important to feel like you're in your Sweet Spot. If you want to live in a tiny cabin by the ocean so you can go surfing any time of the day or night—so be it. If you want a luxurious mansion filled with chandeliers and white carpet (and can afford it), so be it. Your home is your nest, a place that embraces you, a place where you can let go of all pretenses and simply be yourself. You can create a home that makes you feel like you are in your Sweet Spot by creating an environment that reflects your personal style, values, budget, and your dreams.

A dear old friend of mine who I had not seen in years called me up one day as she was travelling north headed towards Nova Scotia from Minnesota, and of course I was hoping she'd pay a visit to our Vermont home, which she did.

The first thing Rebekah said when she arrived at my house was, "Ohhh, your front porch!" As a fellow misplaced Southern gal, we both purchased homes with front porches; it's a nod to our roots, a way to keep us connected to the slow moving way of the south. A common thread between us.

The second thing she said as she walked into the foyer was, "Ohhh, my painting!!" Fifteen years ago, Rebekah came over to my Little Rock home, grabbed a brown paper bag, ripped it open, plopped on the floor with two or three paints and a *National Geographic* for inspiration, and promptly turned out a really cool piece of art. She was about to throw it away, when I asked her if I could have it. Her trash was my treasure, a reminder of Rebekah's artistic talents and why I tend to hang out with artists—I'm inspired by them.

That night Rebekah and her fiancé crawled into the guest bed and tucked themselves into the wooly quilt that she made for me as an engagement present ten years prior. Later, she told me she'd given away all but one of the many quilts she'd made, and what a pleasure it was to sleep under the wooly quilt on a chilly night in Vermont. Perfection.

The porch, the painting, and the quilt are all things that I cherish in my home. They each tell a story and are glimpses of what's important to me. They're part of what make my home feel like I'm in my Sweet Spot.

At the end of Rebekah's visit she told me, "Your home is really *you*"—which I take as a compliment. She said one of the best things about travelling cross-country is getting to see old friends and that you can begin to "catch up" and learn so much about the person and their life just by staying with them in their home. And it's true. Whether you plan it or not, your home does reflect your life. And I have to agree, I love getting a glimpse of the inside of people's homes. I don't love a particular style—I love many styles—but what I love most is learning about the person and what is meaningful to them. And that is what this book is all about!

Answer these questions to find out how you can live in your Sweet Spot at home:

- How do you want to feel in your home?
- What currently makes you feel this way in your home? Why?
- Is there any area of your home that makes you feel uncomfortable, stressed, or that you avoid? Why?
- Do you have a space of your own that feels completely wonderful? What do you do there? If not, can you imagine a space like this in your home?
- What can you do to make your home feel like you are in your Sweet Spot?

THINK ABOUT IT:
What makes your home feel like you are in your Sweet Spot?

CAUTION!! SOUR LIST

There are a few things that will take you right out of your Sweet Spot, leaving you feeling like a sour puss when it comes to your space. Watch out for:

1. **Overspending**—spending more than you can afford on the purchase or decoration of your home is a sure fire way to make you feel stressed, resentful, and could lead to feeling stuck in your life (think opposite of *freedom*).

2. **Dirt!** Having a dirty house is a direct reflection of you. There's a time and place for being a dirty girl, and this isn't it, sugar sweets.

Vintage finds and pops of color reflect the owner's sense of style in this remodeled Vermont barn apartment designed by Sarah Johnson of Kokuun.

3. **Massive Clutter**—I'm all for personalizing a home with family pictures, plenty of art and collections—but clutter often leads to disorganization which blocks creativity and increases inefficiency. You're not in your Sweet Spot if you are yelling, "Where are my damn keys?!" It doesn't mean you have to get rid of your precious stuff, but please, at least organize it.

4. **Overstuffing**—related to Massive Clutter, you don't want to overstuff your home, your closets, drawers, or art space. If you haven't used it in a year, chances are you won't use it all. If your linen closet is overstuffed, it's going to drive you nuts every time the thirty towels fall on your head, right? And do you need thirty towels anyway? Keep the best ones and donate the rest. Somebody will be happy to get those towels for twenty cents apiece and you'll love not being clobbered by a towel waterfall every time you reach into your linen closet. Take this concept and apply it to every nook and cranny of your home. You'll thank me, and yourself for it. Promise.

5. **Think of the *others***. I know this book is about *you* living in *your* Sweet Spot, but here's the thing—if you live with other people it's worth helping them to have a Sweet Spot home too, because when your partner comes in and starts stressing about this or that in the house, or your child doesn't have a proper place to play and get messy—*you* will feel their stress and mess. When thinking about decorating your home to make yourself feel awesome, take a moment and think about the others who share your home. You can even ask them the same questions you are asking yourself: "Honey, what makes you feel awesome in our home?" He/she might surprise you.

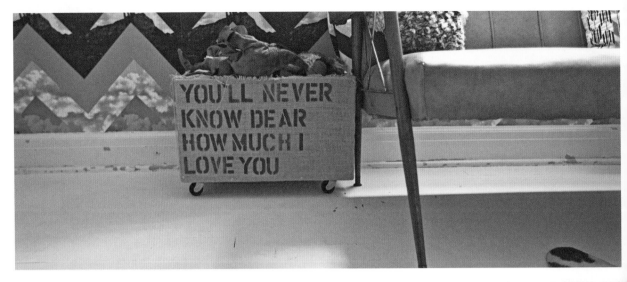

chapter 2

My personal mission is to encourage (and hopefully inspire!) everyone to live fully in their Sweet Spot, whether personal style, home, or career. The saying might be cliché, but it still holds true, "Home is where the heart is."

I wish I could sit down with you over tea and brownies and hear your story. I'd love to help you creatively express yourself in your home and create a space that reflects your unique personal style and values. I'm guessing you already have a good idea of what makes you feel good in a space, you just need a little inspiration and encouragement.

While I'm a huge fan of glossy magazines and home décor books, we all know there's a lot of staging going on. How many times have you thought to yourself "Ok, who is the professional interior designer behind this space?" or "Yeah, I could do that too if I had a giant budget, or a sugar daddy with a big fat wallet."

I wonder what these homes look like once the photographer and stylist have left. I'd love to know, who are these people and how do they really live? Where do they work? Do they have kids? How do they really live with all of those white couches??? Do they really have clean desks with just a lamp, one pretty graphic notebook, a few pens, and a giant vase of peonies?

Ok, so not to judge *at all*. I think it's awesome if you can afford to hire a designer and use their creative skills, and it would be super nice to rely on one big sugar daddy income, it's just that many of us don't live in that reality.

You can look at picture perfect magazines all day long, but I would like to show you some spaces of everyday people sans the super styling that you normally see in a book like this. And don't get me wrong, I love me some fantasy—it's just a lot to live up to, that's all.

Just like unbuttoning a pair of tight jeans, I hope through the following stories and images you can let your breath out a bit and relax knowing that everyday people live in real spaces that are seldom always *perfectly* perfect, but that still feel and look great.

As famous interior designer Nate Berkus says, "We all have a story to tell, and part of the way we do this is through our homes." In the next section, you will become intimate with people who have created a space that reflects their aesthetics and values. You will learn about their occupation, family life, goals, dreams, and desires. I hope that through their stories you will be inspired and encouraged to live fully in your own Sweet Spot.

wood and light

Robin MacArthur: Mother, Writer, Musician
Lives in: Marlboro, Vermont
Describes her Style as: Funky. Luminous. Sustainable.

"I have a claw foot bathtub, which is not at all radical, but in my heart I still dream of being a hairdresser in a trailer in the desert somewhere, and that dream is essential to my understanding of what makes me, me."

—Robin MacArthur

Robin MacArthur, writer and lead singer of Red Heart the Ticker (featured on Prairie Home Companion), built a one-room cabin at age sixteen and has added to it since then, deepening ties to the land and her soul.

A dear friend, Robin is an inspiration in many ways from the music she makes, words she writes, her natural and relaxed parenting, and her devotion to maintaining a sense of self amidst it all. Robin resides with her husband Tyler and two small children in Marlboro, Vermont.

What makes your home feel like you are in your SWEET SPOT?

My home feels like an organic extension of my body and it also tells a story. The story is both my story and the story of this place: my house is built with trees that my dad, husband, and I cut from the land here and had milled into boards and beams. There are tap-holes in my kitchen cabinets from where my parents drilled to collect sap for maple syrup and there are windows salvaged from my grandparents' barn. There is a beautiful, antique slate sink we collected from a neighbor's shed. Every inch of it was built by us (including the foundation and septic system, oy), and with that comes an organic and tactile relationship. It's full of two of my favorite things: wood and light. I can't imagine living anywhere else because this house is me. It's me at sixteen, drinking wine and smoking pot; it's me at twenty-two, driving home from the cities where I lived to curl up next to a wood stove; and it's me at thirty-four, a mother to two children, one of whom was born on the pine floor of the upstairs bedroom.

How does the creation of your home reflect you and your lifestyle?
Our house has been an ad hoc creation that seems to reflect the stages of my
life to a tee. It began with a small, one room cabin I built with my dad when
I was sixteen. It was breezy and full of salvaged windows and sat on crooked
stumps and piles of rock. I would go there to drink wine with friends and
sleep with boyfriends and write poetry and smoke cigarettes by myself. It was
perfection. At twenty-five my boyfriend (now husband Ty) and I were living in
New York but wanted to have a place to return to for all seasons of the year, so
we added on another small rectangle that was insulated.

It was still funky—the electricity came from a two-hundred-foot extension cord
that ran through the woods, the windows were old breezy single-panes, and
there was no running water, just an outhouse and a stinky bucket under the
sink. Also perfection! We spent summers and a few winters there, then moved
to Philadelphia. At twenty-nine we decided we wanted to have a baby and that
we wanted to raise that baby in the woods on the land where I was born. So
addition number three: this time with a septic system and real electricity and
some double-pane windows. We just got a dishwasher, which makes our house
verifiably bourgeois.

This amazing farm style sink was found in a neighbor's barn; patches of locally milled wood and
Vermont concrete add spunk and variety to the countertops.

You are a writer and musician. How does your home reflect your creative passions and values?

Books. I love books, and read probably six in a month. I have an MFA in fiction writing and though I usually devour fiction, the last four months I've been after much more lyrical things, tied to what's real. My favorite poem right now is Olds's "New Mother," which if you've ever given birth, might mean something to you. "... the first time you're broken, you don't know you'll be healed again, better than before."

Although I have many musician friends for whom music is the primary thing of their lives, it's not at all like that for me. In order to rid myself of the anxiety of wondering how I can make room for all my passions, I've starting thinking of my life as a quilt of sorts, which is, fittingly, a very feminine art form. I'm currently thinking of it as a log cabin design, with repeated colors and patterns. Music is one of those patterns and colors in my life. Playing it around the house might be a deep gray color—I was raised in a family of folkies and

so a banjo and a guitar around the wood stove feel like a cat purring on one's lap. Performing is the bright red one—the time when I get to don tight jeans and cowboy boots and eyeliner and leave my kids with my parents and stand up under lights and feel radically young again. The rest of my life is quite earthy and domestic—a vegetable garden, mothering, chickens, cooking, writing

while my children sleep. For those reasons I desperately need those splashes of Red Heart the Ticker.

What's one thing that makes your heart sing?
The indomitable spirit of my daughter makes me unbearably happy. As she and I like to say to one another, "It's just too much! I just love you too much!"

How does your home reflect *you*, your dreams, aspirations, and desires?

My grandmother, Margaret MacArthur, had a heart-shaped pink Jacuzzi-style bathtub in the upstairs bathroom of her muted, antiques-filled 1803 farmhouse. That bathtub has always exemplified to me the wonderful idiosyncrasies of her untamable heart. I have a claw-foot bathtub, which is not at all radical, but in my heart I still dream of being a hairdresser in a trailer in the desert somewhere, and that dream is essential to my understanding of what makes me, me.

Listen to Robin's music at Red Heart the Ticker, rhtt.net
Read her blog at Woodbird, woodbirdandthensome.blogspot.com

let the sun shine

Nor Toma: Public Relations Guru, Fashionista, Dreamer
Lives in: Sweden
Describes her Style as: Bohemian. Embracing. Dreamy.

"Imagine a folklore rainbow that exploded and that all the magical pieces within it fell apart and landed in my apartment."

—Nor Toma

Head of PR at Monki, a Swedish fashion and lifestyle brand, Nor Toma infuses her own style with a bit of fashion-influenced whimsy combined with vintage thrift store finds to create her Sweet Spot home in Sweden.

You are head of PR for Monki. How has your work in PR and fashion influenced your sense of style in your home?
I suppose my work has given me good insight and appreciation for designer pieces that come through the fashion houses, but I am also able to find joy in found objects and treasures. I think it's interesting to combine high end pieces like a Maison Martin Margiela bottle lamp with a unique second hand store find.

How does your home reflect your lifestyle, values, and what's important to you?
My home is structured chaos. It's an overload of impressions, but all is very carefully placed out. Imagine a folklore rainbow

that exploded and that all the magical pieces within it fell apart and landed in my apartment. Decorating is a meditative act; it's a way for me to draw out my feelings and thoughts and transform them into interior constellations.

How have you created the space you love on a budget you can afford?

Whenever I get the chance to travel, I take the time to visit odd and off location antique shops. Or as I did when I found my vintage butterfly chair in ornamented leather; I was in Berlin and simply googled "butterfly chair" and on some German website I found what looked to be an old lady selling this beautiful chair. I called up and the old lady turned out to be a gorgeous musician who picked me up in his car and we drove to his garage full of unique and crazy designer pieces. I packed my backpack with as much as I could carry, paid almost nothing, and then took the flight home.

What's one thing that makes your heart sing?

I love *love* (I guess that's cliché, but it's true). And magic. And oddities. And I adore long-distance travels.

Nor at home in her beautiful butterfly chair.

How does your home reflect your dreams, aspirations, and desires?
My home is a dream—my dream. When I'm there I could be in a trailer in Joshua Tree having kombucha, in a bungalow in Sri Lanka surrounded by macramé hanging plants and patchouli, or at a coffee bar in New York flipping through a nice coffee table book. Anything is possible in my space and there is nothing there that could pop my daydream.

Are you living in your Sweet Spot?
For sure, it's my serene escape from reality.

What tips do you have to help others create their own Sweet Spot home?
Never get anything when you're stressed out or in a bad mood. Only get things when you have a good energy. The energy will be transferred to the piece you get and then gleam blissfully in your own home.

Anything else you'd like readers to know about?
Let the sun shine.

a love affair with new orleans

Erin Gandy: Mother, Grad Student, Airbnb Host
Lives in: New Orleans, Louisiana
Describes her Style as: Peaceful. Functional. Welcoming.

Embrace project and budget limitations. These limitations often spark the coolest ideas and most interesting spaces.
—Erin Gandy

Erin Gandy shares her very sweet shotgun home in NOLA with her husband Greg and three year old son, Wyatt. Her family loves New Orleans for its French Creole architecture, as well as its cross-cultural and multilingual heritage. Erin explains she moved into the home post-Katrina to experience the rebirth of her favorite city. The air itself shapes the patina and texture of her home, adding history and charm that one can only experience in NOLA.

She loves the illusion that her home looks like a tiny dollhouse from the front, but once you enter the space it magically expands, each room offering a new surprise as you walk the length of the home. Working with a tight budget, Erin updated the space with items found on Craigslist or other used furniture that needed a little TLC. She modified a separate, private space in the back

of the home that she rents exclusively on Airbnb. This income, plus income earned when the house was featured on HBO's *Treme*, has allowed her to quit her job and pursue a degree in occupational therapy. Erin feels that her home is not only a space she loves for herself and family, but it also gives her financial freedom to return to school, spend more time with her son, and live more fully in her Sweet Spot.

How does your home reflect you and your unique personal style?
I'm definitely an old house person, so I would not have considered buying something new. The house is about a hundred years old and I like that it's full of history and scars. It's weathered many storms and reconfigurations, but it has survived. It's inspiring to think of your home being strong in that way. Even when it flooded due to Hurricane Katrina and took in several feet of water, the bones of the home stood up to the storm. It's pretty amazing that the floor didn't buckle with all that water sitting there. But it was strong and it made it, and that's what makes it special.

Erin's tips: If there is something I don't like in my home, I prefer to work with it, rather than immediately rip it out. For example, I didn't like my kitchen cabinets, but instead of getting new ones, I painted them myself. You'd be surprised how much you can do with paint. I've found that having limitations on your project can bring about the best creative results.

> People don't operate at their optimal level when they have to be in a space that's not well thought out, that's disorderly or ugly. We've all had the experience of working someplace ugly, and it's awful. It affects the way you feel.

How does your home décor reflect you and who you are?

I believe that you should make a home beautiful and pleasant for the people who live there, not to impress other people. I'm not one of those people who cleans for company. It really matters to me that my home is beautiful because this is the space we use everyday. Your home is like your own personal church—this is our sacred space and that's really important to me.

That said, it's more important that my home be welcoming and functional than perfect. A house is for living in. We jump on the bed, we play ball inside and break china, and we have glitter projects on the floor and all of that. We use the house. I don't want a place where you feel like you can't sit down or make a mess.

How does your home reflect your creative passions and/or your values?

I enjoy painting and drawing but realistically I don't have time for that right now, so I use homemaking as a creative outlet. Creating a lovely home environment benefits us all and I think that's an important thing for my son to learn as well.

I also just really enjoy the process of setting up a space. It feels like play, like one of those activities that you can lose yourself in. I felt like that when we first moved in and I still feel like that when I'm rethinking a room or getting the garden ready for the next season. I just immerse myself in the project, almost like a meditative practice, and hours pass without me even noticing.

I think of shotgun homes as little cakes. The woodwork on the front of the house is called "gingerbread" for a reason!

How does your home reflect your dreams, aspirations, and/or desires?

Dreams: It was a dream of mine for many years to live in NOLA in a shotgun house. I like the fact that the exterior shows so little of what's within. You have this tiny little dollhouse exterior; I'd say I live in cupcake—that's what it looks like. There's this little dollhouse entry and then you come inside and the whole space expands before you. I also like the concept of not wasting space with hallways.

Within the family, we aren't particularly private people. I don't mind the fact that people walk through my bedroom to get to my kitchen. To me a home is all living space, so I don't feel the need to have really private spaces that people don't go into. It's all functional living space.

"What looks like a tiny little cupcake house opens up into an expansive space that just keeps going. Each room offers another surprise."

There are shotgun-style homes in other areas of the country, but the ones in NOLA have a particular look. Originally built for the lower class workers, builders still added detailed woodwork normally associated with the Victorian era. Also, the homes in NOLA are always under assault by water. It's in the air. Once a year we have to pressure wash this house or it will be black with stuff growing on it. We are just always fighting decay, but that's what gives the homes their unique and weathered patina.

Aspirations: I aspire to settle and stay. I'm not planning to move again. The concept of expanding this home is more attractive than changing locations. I aspire to create memories in this home, a place my son will remember fondly.

Desires: I desire to experience the sensations and feeling of home more fully. It's such a sensual place—the tastes, the smells, and the way the air feels.

What makes your home feel like you are living in your Sweet Spot?

When I think of how we discovered our Sweet Spot, I think about my garden. When you're planning a garden, you think you know what a plant likes and so you put it in a place where it has the right soil, sun, and space to thrive. Sometimes it works beautifully and sometimes the plant just doesn't take. Sometimes you can't know whether something will work until you try it.

We tried out a few locations before moving to NOLA, but I feel like now we've found our place. We'd thought about moving here for years, but now that we have a child, it feels right to be near our extended family. My husband is doing work he loves here. Everything is in place. I've gone back to school for a new career.

I don't want to see my kid on the side; I want have a career and lifestyle that allows me the freedom to be with my child, create a loving home, go hear good music, be with friends, and enjoy the city. It took me a decade to figure out how to fit all these things together in my life.

Just like the plant that finds itself in the right place in the garden, we've found our place and we are thriving. **We are in our Sweet Spot for sure.**

Erin's guest space is rented on Airbnb, but also serves as a quiet place for Erin to escape to her own little "pretend vacation spot."

Do you have a special, most favorite place in your house?

That's a hard one. I like the front room because I love the long window to the porch. It's also where we put our tree and where Santa comes. It's our family space, a place to relax. But I also like being in my guest space, like a little getaway. There are no chores in that room, if you know what I mean. It's our little pretend vacation spot.

How has renting the guest space helped you and your family live in your Sweet Spot?

We use Airbnb to rent the guest space in the back of our home, which includes a bedroom, bathroom, and private entrance. The cool thing about Airbnb is that it allows you to operate on such a small scale. It provides a golden opportunity for us to generate some income using the space we have and it's manageable for me while I'm a student.

Having this income is the difference between just barely surviving and being comfortable. We have to be careful now that I'm in school because it's an income reduction, but with the rental income it's not so tight. If we need something, we can buy it. If we want to go have a date or out for a drink, we can do that.

It's been a real lifesaver and we'll continue to rent out the space even after grad school in order to pay down student loans or get a new tub that my entire body will fit in. That's my next dream.

Making a trip to the big easy? You can stay in Erin's special guest suite, but book early, as this cutie pie cupcake fills up fast! airbnb.com/rooms/684584.

Sarah feels like she's in her Sweet Spot when soaking up the sun and relaxing on one of her favorite couches.

things aren't precious; people are

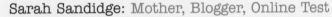

Sarah Sandidge: Mother, Blogger, Online Test Grader, Freelance Writer

Lives in: Springfield, Missouri

Describes her Style as: Eclectic. Cheery. Cozy.

"My home feels like an extension of me."

—Sarah Sandidge

Sarah Sandidge is a gypsy at heart who loves to surround herself with bold colors and textures against a nice, crisp background of white. She appreciates that things come and go and that the real value in her home are the people who reside inside. Her eclectic, cheery home is full of thrifted finds that mirror her casual, yet fun lifestyle.

Tell me a bit about you . . .
I live in the Midwest in a not so very exciting town, but it's slowly become home. The great thing about where I live is that even though it's smallish, there are tons of old houses here and interesting architecture. I couldn't live somewhere that had no history!

I have an online job grading standardized tests (yawn!). I also do a bit of freelance writing and professional blogging at *Lovely Chaos* and *A Birth Story*. But my main job at the

moment is taking care of my two sweet babies (Lula Mae, 4, and Diesel, 2) until they're in school full time. I'm able to do that because of my husband's wonderful job as the national director of marketing for his company. I appreciate how hard he works so I can stay home with our kids.

As far as hobbies go, I read every spare chance I get. I love to dream about renovating my house (yes, this is a legitimate hobby because my dreams turn into my husband's handiwork, which is his hobby!). I also enjoy sewing, decorating, and spending time with my family.

How does your home creatively reflect who you are and your lifestyle?
It seems cliché these days, but I would consider my home perfectly eclectic, and I feel that fits with my personality and the lifestyle of my family very well. I'm a wanderer at heart, a gypsy. But my husband is not. He is solid and stable, a rock. So our home is clean and neat and sometimes sparse (for Jay's sake), but there are lots of different styles and colors interwoven together (for my sake).

It took me a long time to realize that possessions aren't and shouldn't be precious. Jay helped me realize that. It's a very freeing and peaceful way to view life. Most of our furniture is old, used, and was purchased cheaply. I want to enjoy what we're doing on the furniture more than the furniture itself. Before we had kids I purchased some gorgeous folding chairs from Anthropologie that were covered with brightly covered fabric. It was a splurge, an indulgence, and I was madly in love with them. But once the kids came, and then their little friends with grubby hands and faces came, I became obsessed with keeping them clean. We'd put them away when company came over. It seemed so silly and ridiculous! So I finally sold them. I don't want to live that way, where I'm more concerned about spills than the conversation I'm having with friends.

Our house is and feels lived in. Don't get me wrong—I love nice things and search high and low for nice things that are cheap. But because they're cheap, if they get ruined, it's not a big deal; it's an excuse to go shopping! And when my kids and all their friends are quite a bit older and no longer in danger of frequent spills and dirty hands, I'll probably buy some really nice things and enjoy them thoroughly until the grandkids come!

You describe your blog, *Lovely Chaos*, as a "lifestyle" blog with a bit of "crafty" and "kids" tied in. Tell me more . . .
When I first started my blog, *Lovely Chaos*, I imagined it being glamorous, filled with kids' fashion and home décor and mind-blowing DIYs. But after a while I got tired of trying to "keep up" in the blog world. I just wanted to keep track of our lives and things that interested me via my blog. It's become somewhat of a public journal of our lives. I love writing more than anything else. So I wanted to stop focusing on perfect pictures and just write about what I wanted to write about. Of course that doesn't help you win any popularity contests, but that's not my goal. So I'm okay with that!

With all that being said, I just purchased my first professional camera and do intend to start taking better pictures for my blog. No matter how amazing my writing is, people enjoy the quick, visual aspect of a blog more than anything else. If I'm going to continue and be successful at all, I'll simply have to follow suit!

Have you done many home renovations? What was your favorite project and how did you manage it with two small children?
I feel like I've been doing home renovations my whole life! That may be an exaggeration, but renovations definitely have taken up a large majority of our married lives. I love old homes, and I love giving them a facelift. The home pictured here is our fourth home, and we've done renovations to all of them. We actually bought a brand new home once that no one else had lived in to give Jay a "break" from renovations. But the very first thing we did was tear out a wall in our bonus room to create a built-in office! Our friends thought we were crazy; it's just in our blood.

Sarah designed this play kitchen for her children using vintage toy appliances and real countertops!

This current house was the most difficult because we have small children. I was five weeks pregnant when we moved in and Lula was almost two. It was nightmarish for a while. I had a rough pregnancy and couldn't really help Jay much. We were at each other a lot. So the projects weren't really fun until after Diesel was born and we were out of the newborn phase. It was definitely rough doing dirty work, not having a kitchen, having floors redone, etc. with little ones running around. Thankfully our kids are super flexible and adaptable. They don't have much of a choice! But I think they're both going to be very easy-going because of our craziness.

Get creative with your child's room, adding whimsy like in Diesel's room, age two.

My favorite project was decorating once Jay was finished with all the major renovations! I waited two years to really start decorating. The kids' rooms were probably the most fun. Diesel's room was the first one that really felt complete, finished. I loved just standing in his room once it was done. I could breathe deeply in his room and look around without seeing unfinished projects.

Lula's room took quite a bit longer. I had actually decorated it completely at one point, made curtains, painted furniture, etc., only to change it completely later. I wanted her to have a room she could grow into, that would last at least through her preteen years, but that would also be whimsical and magical. I took a lot of time looking at pictures online, sifting through magazines, looking at hundreds of paint samples, and scouring Craigslist for the perfect furniture.

I was so overwhelmed by her room because I wanted it to be perfect. After posting my dilemma on my blog, a good friend offered some advice that I will

If your child loves a certain color, consider painting the ceiling that color, like Lula's purple ceiling. It's easy to change later, but will greatly satisfy your child in the meantime!

remember forever. She said to just do one big thing at a time. Don't try to do the whole room at once or even picture the whole room at once (which is exactly what I was doing!). Start with something big that you're sure about. Then take a break, step back, and think about the next step.

That was the best decorating advice I've ever received, and that's exactly what I did. I knew I wanted to paint Lula's ceiling purple. I was one hundred percent sure about that. So I did that first and forgot about everything else until that was done. In the end, I think her room turned out beautifully. It's magical and sweet, but she'll easily be able to grow up in it.

How does your home reflect your values and what's important to you?

The casualness of our home reflects an important family value that things aren't precious; people are. We want our family, friends, and guests to all feel welcome, loved, at peace, and relaxed when they enter our home. While I love nice furniture and sophisticated styles, I want guests to feel like they can kick off their shoes and curl up on any piece of furniture. At the same time, I like pretty things. I want my surroundings to be beautiful and am very particular about styles when I decorate. My house is "put together." Nothing was chosen haphazardly or randomly even though it's very eclectic. I think people feel that when they come to our house as well.

What inspires you?

So many things inspire me: friends' homes, magazines, Pinterest, blogs, nature, my own thoughts and dreams in my head. I find my inspiration in these things for decorating and renovating.

But my biggest inspiration for my life goals is found in my children. I've always been a dreamer more than a doer. I've had big dreams my whole life, but rarely accomplished any of them because it was more fun to dream than do, and honestly I was always afraid of failure. But when my daughter was born, that all changed. A fire was sparked in me to be and do great things for her sake. I wanted her view of me later in life to be one of a mother who dreamed big but then acted on those dreams. Even if I fail at everything I try, at least I tried.

How does your home reflect your dreams, aspirations, and desires?

My dream home is a place where I can live my life to the fullest, dream my dreams, and love my family. Because we renovated our home to suit our tastes, it is truly the sweetest spot in the world. My home feels like an extension of me. Though I strive to be less materialistic, to want less, and need less, my surroundings really affect my mood and motivation. So it's important that my home reflects my personality. I feel like we live simply and aren't attached to our "things," but we also love the atmosphere we've created. You can create a rich, wonderful, personal atmosphere without breaking the bank.

Do you have a favorite place in your home that makes you feel like you are thriving in your Sweet Spot?

I have two favorite places in my house. Both are favorites for the same reasons. One of my Sweet Spots is on my yellow couch in the living room. The other is on my yellow couch in our master suite. I'm a couch girl, a lounger. I've always thought I would've fit in very well in the Roman era where they lounged on couches while eating. That is me through and through! I love to be comfortable and cozy. I love to be able to curl my feet up, lay my head back, and snuggle under a blanket. So my couches are favorite pieces of furniture to sit on.

White walls in the kitchen allow for other pops of color in your cabinets. Try using fabric and textures in the kitchen, such as Sarah's wool rug and cabinet curtain, to soften the space and make it even more inviting.

But I also love these two places because they are the sunniest and cheeriest spots in the house. I can sit in the corner of the couch and see out windows, and also see the beautiful room I've created. These are peaceful spots. Spots where children and their toys rarely enter. Spots where I can dream and rest and be rejuvenated. This is where I read, where I eat when I'm alone, where I nap, where I think.

I never thought I'd decorate with yellow furniture, and when you're buying thrift or flea market goods, sometimes you just get what you get. But I'm so glad I found these two brightly colored couches because they reflect the warmth of the sun and make those spots that much sweeter.

What tips do you have to help others create their own Sweet Spot home on a budget?

When renovating on a budget, the biggest money saver is doing the renovations yourself or finding friends who can help. My husband did most of the work himself. Of course when you go this route, you give up lots of time.

Use a variety of textures and styles to add to your eclectic look, as Sarah did in her bathroom.

So it's important to decide if time or money is more important, and that may vary for each project depending on your skill set.

There's also the cost of materials. There is a huge range of cost when it comes to materials. You can buy cheap laminate flooring or the most expensive reclaimed wood floors from overseas. But there are definitely ways to get exactly what you want, or at least close, for a good price if you're willing to look around (like on Craigslist for example) and be patient. Love those metal cabinets in a kitchen you saw in *Dwell* magazine? Keep looking around on Craigslist and someone just might be giving them away.

As far as decorating on a budget, there's nothing better than flea markets, thrift stores, Craigslist, and garage sales! Almost every item in my home has come from one of those places. The key is patience, flexibility, and diligence. When I'm searching for certain pieces of furniture, I look on Craigslist every day and hit thrift stores and flea markets as much as possible. Sometimes you'll find something you didn't even know you were looking for!

It's also helpful to at least have a raw vision in mind. If you just go out searching without some kind of idea, you'll end up with pieces you don't really want or that don't fit. I've done this numerous times. Of course the great thing about buying something cheap is that it doesn't hurt to get rid of it again!

Find Sarah online at LovelyChaos.typepad and A BirthStoryBlog.com.

vintage, white and random

Janae Hardy: Mother, Blogger, Freelance Writer
Lives in: Springfield, Missouri
Describes her Style as: Random. White. Vintage.

"Your decor is like your personality or clothing style ... do what you love and be confident about your choices."

—Janae Hardy

Photographer and stay-at-home mom extraordinaire, Janae Hardy describes her home as random, vintage, and white. Influenced by her creative friends and neighbors in Rountree, Janae documents the uber-stylish homes in her neighborhood on her blog, *The Itsy Bitsy House.*

Tell me a bit about you ...

My name is Janae Hardy and I'm married to a super sweet man and we have three children. I am a freelance photographer, but also a stay-at-home mom. We have lots of fun with our kids and they keep us busy! Professionally, I photograph people, spaces, and sometimes a wedding here and there. Being a photographer is my dream job. I'm so grateful I get to be a mom and work at the same time!

How does your home creatively reflect who you are and your lifestyle?

Sporadic and random! I can fully admit that our home doesn't match and it's not completely cohesive, but that's what I love about it. It reflects our family. By not sticking to certain rules, I can go to flea markets and pick out

whatever I like and not worry that it won't "match" the rest of the house. By not putting myself in a decor style "box," I am able to have more freedom decorating. I think the most important aspect of decorating is to do what you like. That's it, plain and simple. Don't follow all the trends because you feel a pressure to be cool; just do what you love. I love going into people's homes and seeing how they decorate. There is such a psychology about it! I think

"The sea foam green desk in my master bedroom costs $30 on Craigslist. I sanded it and painted it with an oil based paint. It's so glossy and perfect with that paint! " —Janae

your decor is like your personality or clothing style . . . do what you love and be confident about your choices.

How does your passion for photography and for your home intermingle?

I love light and composition. Every room in our home is white. I love the way the light bounces off the white walls. Also, it photographs beautifully! That is a plus in my book. I have somewhat of an obsession when it comes to visual balance. When I am taking a picture, balance plays a big part for me. I once had a painting teacher who said if you squint your eyes while you look at your painting, you will be able to determine the visual balance better. I do this with my home. I think it's important to make sure your eye is constantly bouncing off elements in my home.

"The pink/red nightstand in our bedroom was found for $15 at an antique store and was *so* ugly with brown lacquered wood and faux gold knobs. I spray painted it and now I love it!" —Janae

I've seen several home tours on *Itsy Bitsy House* and *Smile & Wave* with a similar aesthetic, which I adore (we are featuring one of them here—the home of Sarah Sandidge). Do you ladies live in the same neighborhood? Friends? Tell me more.

Yes, Sarah and I are friends. We go to church together and our children are friends. We can talk about creativity and decorating for hours—we love it. The other homes that were featured on blogs were friends and also my neighbors in Rountree—I think of it as the decorating Mecca! We're constantly inspired because we're surrounded by such beautiful spaces! It's like a jewel box of the most beautiful homes with super creative owners. My secret wish is to one day photograph a book of our neighborhood. It's full of the most inspiring spaces.

Can you tell me about the remodeling of your attic space? How did you manage it with two small children and another on the way? Any tips on reducing the stress?

We renovated our attic when I was thirty-three weeks pregnant and finished when I was thirty-nine weeks. It was a speedy process. We decided to renovate and make the upstairs the master bedroom. It turned out better than we imagined! A wonderful builder really made everything come to life when it

The pedestal sink was another Craigslist find for just $40.

came to our original plans. It was tough having small children during this process. When renovating, my tips for having small children are . . . live somewhere else for a while. Having machinery, nails, dust, and dry wall lying around was scary. Our house was small enough that the kids couldn't get away from the mess, so we had to leave. If we had a home with a wing untouched from renovations, we would have lived there; the size of our house just forced us to move out for a few weeks until the dust settled. Also, the mess was worse than I ever expected. I was told to be prepared, but nothing really prepared me for the true demo process! But keep a positive attitude because the outcome is *so* worth it.

How does your home reflect your values and what's important to you?

Family is very important to me. My husband and I strive to make our home a safe haven for our children. We want them to grow up knowing they have a mom and dad who are crazy about them. We also want our home to be comfortable for them. I think if the decor was stuffy or fancy, they would feel a disconnect. I also want my kids to grow up being inspired and creative. When it comes to our home, I'll let my daughter help me rearrange or decorate—she

feels empowered and happy when she does. I love seeing what she comes up with when I let her loose and decorate.

What inspires you?

My children. They have opened my eyes to so much. They have such a fresh and unhindered perspective on life. They see the simple beauty in everything. I think a child's point of view is profound and being with them helps me keep my eyes open to everything around me. I also love decor books, magazines, and design blogs.

Do you have a favorite place in your home that makes you feel like you are thriving in your Sweet Spot?

Our newly renovated attic is my favorite. It has a distinct ambiance when you walk up the stairs. Each night after a long day, I walk up the stairs and smile.

The whole room is so inviting and happy. I think that is what a master bedroom should be, an escape and haven.

What tips do you have to help others create their own Sweet Spot home on a budget?

Go to local flea markets, thrift stores, and garage sales! Ninety-five percent of our home décor is from secondhand stores and tag sales. That said, you should try and buy quality pieces. If something has good bones, chances are it just needs a little love to look great again. Don't be afraid to reupholster or refinish a piece of furniture. There are resources online that have helped me with many DIY projects around the house.

Most little girls would love to have a bright pink room, but Juliet's daughter gently rebels by choosing soft pastels and white in her bedroom.

sustainable design with pops of hot pink

Juliet Cuming: Designer, Director, Dreamer, Mother
Lives in: East Dummerston, Vermont
Describes her Style as: Colorful. Sculptural. Biodegradable.

"When we started building our home we had no idea how it would end up, or how we would end up paying for it, but life has evolved to support the dreams we had and I feel that the universe has supported us in our journey."

—Juliet Cuming

The home of Juliet Cuming in rural Vermont offers a stylish, modern, and healthy home that's family friendly. Built in 1996, this straw bale home is both solar and wind powered. Juliet and her husband designed their home using age-old and alternative building technologies to create a structure that is healthy, beautiful, economically viable, and sustainable.

Tell me a bit about you and your family.
I was born in Brussels, Belgium but raised in Manhattan, and my husband David is a born and bred New Yorker. My parents were English and French so I thought of myself as being more European than American. I was very affected by the European idea of taking old things and making them feel new. I was raised on second hand stuff—furniture, clothes, everything. My mom created a great deal of elegance with things she found at thrift stores and antique shops. I loved (and still love)

the way that Europeans take their very old buildings and make them modern. They do not feel the need to make everything "authentic" or "period." I am glad that Americans are finally catching up and getting comfortable with the idea of putting a modern interior inside an old looking house.

David and I met in 1989 when we were both working in the film industry; I was a fashion designer and was doing costumes for bands and working on music videos. I had just started directing music videos when we met, and David was a cinematographer. We shared an interest in "modern" design, and we both favored spare, colorful design.

We left New York City in 1991 to change our lives and ultimately to raise our family—Hunter was born in 1996 and Luna in 2005. Since our kids were little, we've been building our house and studio workspace and as a result I am guessing that neither of them will *ever* choose to build a house!

We live and work in our home, running a photo archive that surrounds us with the beautiful photography of Mark Shaw (David's father), who was a fashion, advertising, and celebrity photographer of the 1950s. For fifteen years both kids were at home with us because we homeschooled them. Because we were part of a big homeschooling group in our area, we often had kids over at our house playing and learning. Our house is very kid-friendly and colorful.

In 2011 both our kids went to school for the first time, our son to tenth grade, our daughter to first grade—it has been a big adjustment that we are still getting used to.

How does your home reflect who you are and your lifestyle?
My home is a reflection of both my (and my husband David's) strengths and our weaknesses. It is an ever-evolving snapshot of our mental, physical, and financial health! In the beginning our goal was to create a totally natural, healthy, locally sourced and biodegradable home. (The details of our commitment can be found on our website earthsweethome.com). We invested in our solar and wind system before we built anything else because we wanted

The upstairs hallway acts as an art gallery, full of photos taken by the famous photographer, Mark Shaw, David's father.

to make sure we had homegrown power both throughout the building process and once we had finished building. The house needed to be all-natural because I had become chemically sensitive and could not tolerate plastic foams and any of the chemical odors that were still found in building materials in the mid 1990s. I had become ill after several very busy years living and working in New York City. I am still not sure if my immune system was destroyed by chemicals I encountered in the garment industry, repeated infections and rounds of antibiotics and other medications, too much early success and burning the candle at both ends, or most likely a combination of all these factors, but by the age of twenty-four I was really a mess and did not see how I was going to survive the rest of my life.

I started on a path of natural healing and after a while I began to feel better, but I was still vulnerable and weak and the hard shell that I had built up to survive in a place like New York City was dissolving. I could not stay in the city and continue to get well, so I had to leave. I tried various places and

eventually David and I settled on a rural life in the culturally vibrant but still small town-like area of Southern Vermont. We are not here by accident nor did work lead us here. We chose the area first and then had to figure out how to make a life here.

So, the first important thing about our home is that it was a place to heal and it comes from a very idealistic and hopeful set of goals. But up against that is the fact that while we were building we were limited by several factors: I was still relatively sick (though getting better!), we had a new baby, David is not a builder or carpenter or particularly good with tape measures etc., and our funds were very limited! So we had a big dream, but not enough money to make it happen. Hence our home is actually very simple and made out of fairly inexpensive local materials. And our home evolved over many years since we could only do things when we could afford them.

Some of the features of our home evolved out of mistakes, some of our choices of materials were limited by our financial situation, and the fact that many outside people helped us build the house means that some parts of the house are rustic and roughly done while others are quite careful and finished. Luckily straw bale is a forgiving and organic material that allows for all these inconsistencies and in fact lends itself to the mix of rough and smooth.

An important thing that you need to know when you visit our house is that my husband *likes* bright pink. So if you see a lot of bright pink (which you will in my house!) you need to understand that that was a mutually agreed upon choice. My husband's love for pink, and his appreciation of design in general, is one of the reasons we have been able to remain married. How could I ever let go of a man who loves pink as much as I do?

You and your husband both used to live and work in NYC and now you both work from home in rural Vermont. How does your current work and home life feed your Sweet Spot?

I always knew I would be an entrepreneur. I started my first fashion design company when I was eighteen and for the next several years was always running a business out of a series of small, dark, cramped apartments, my sewing machines and rolls of fabric usually fighting for space with my bed! So working from home is natural to me and now I have a beautiful, spacious home to work from.

Working from home also allowed me to homeschool my two children, something I did not plan on beforehand, but which was a natural progression of the home birthing, breastfeeding, attachment parenting, all natural lifestyle I had embarked on. By running a family business from home I have had

I THINK IT IS GOOD FOR KIDS TO SEE AND UNDERSTAND HOW THEIR PARENTS MAKE A LIVING.

the flexibility to give my kids the time they have needed from me, while also enabling them to see what "work" requires. Having kids see and understand the demands of moneymaking is the part of homeschooling or "attachment" parenting that often gets lost. I think it is good for kids to see and understand how their parents make a living.

The lifestyle of a homeschooler and of a home-based business means that you are "always at work" or "always at school." This might seem strange from a twentieth century perspective where generally parents and kids lived separate and somewhat mysterious lives, but prior to the twentieth century the lines between home, work, and school were similarly joined. In this century, mobile communication has allowed us to work *anywhere*, which is both a blessing and a curse. For those of us who are homebodies and who have beautiful homes that we want to spend time in, it makes life a lot more holistic. And an investment in our home is also an investment in our work!

Juliet and David added the studio where they work side by side in their photo archiving business. Downstairs, a private apartment is available for when family and friends pay a visit.

What's one thing that makes your heart sing?

I love pink, bright colors, and exuberance. I also love looking out on nature and feeling connected to both the Earth and the people who lived in closer connection to the Earth. I am not a person who loves to hike or climb mountains—I'd rather look at them! But I love living in a place where Mother Nature is in charge! And I love being able to use the things found in nature to create a home that reflects my love of all that is bright and cheerful. Nature created the colors I love so much and I bring them into my home so I can enjoy them all year round.

How does your home reflect *you*, your dreams, aspirations, and desires?

I would say that my home is the physical embodiment of a dream that I had when I was sick and unhappy living in New York City. My home is the embodiment of hope and of healing. My home tells me and others that dreams

Juliet's light-filled bathroom lends itself to relaxation and comfort. The sitting chair is covered in zebra striped towels, a funky and fun way to add comfort and warmth.

can come true. When we started building our home we had *no* idea how it would end up, or how we would end up paying for it, but life has evolved to support the dreams we had and I feel that the universe has supported us in our journey.

Do you have a favorite place in your home that makes you feel like you are thriving in your Sweet Spot?

My whole house is filled with Sweet Spots. I love sitting at the dining table and looking out on the field and the trees; I love coming up the stairs and looking at my hallway that was the result of all kinds of mistakes (the stairs were put in a different place than expected, there were strange walls and shapes to deal with, an ugly chimney etc.). I love my bedroom and now, finally, after eighteen years, my little bedroom balcony that looks over my garden and over the living roof. I love my office and the way it looks out on nature. I love my garden and

all the landscaping that we finally did after years of not being able to afford it or even realizing how important it was and what a difference it would make.

What's one bit of advice you'd give others who want to create their own Sweet Spot home?

Don't be afraid to have a dream and to dream *big* and *bright*. Be bold, take chances. Right now I think I may have gone over the top with color and pattern in my living room, so this year we might dial it back a bit, but I don't have any regrets about any of the decisions I have made. I love that my home is wild and fun.

What tips do you have for people who might be on a budget?

I won't stay "start small" because sometimes you need to start big and fill in over time (that's what we did—we built a big shell and finished bit by bit) but I will say *start* because you are more likely to finish something once you have started it. If you wait until all the conditions are perfect, you will never get anywhere. But if you are on a budget you must be willing to take several years to reach your goal.

Remember that everything costs twice what you think it will. Be prepared to do a lot of research and hard work and you may even really struggle to create your beautiful home. But great things in life are not always easy! Have faith that it will all work out in the end.

Also, do *not* make the mistake I did—remember that landscaping makes a *huge* impact and if you do that you might find you don't have to make as many other changes.

Now at age forty-eight (what???) my home and my life are a lot different than they were when I started at age thirty. My dreams have come to fruition and problems were solved in ways I never imagined. Don't assume it will all go according to plan, and be grateful that it doesn't! It will probably turn out better than you planned.

Learn more about Juliet and David's home at earthsweethome.com and their amazing photo archive business markshawphoto.com.

renaissance man

Daniel Kornguth: Artist, Musician, Comic Stripper,
Builder, Event Organizer, and the List Goes On . . .
Lives in: Brattleboro, Vermont
Describes his Style as: Fearless. Intentional.
Comfortable.

*"When you walk into my house you can see that I love beauty.
I enjoy sharing my space with guests as a place to exchange
ideas, support one another and foster creativity."*

—Daniel Kornguth

I met Daniel at one of his epic dance parties in a massive
warehouse full of art studios when I first moved to Vermont.
I had a huge rhinestone peacock pinned to my hip. He
asked if I wanted to smoke a cigarette and take a ride on his
motorcycle. Immediate friends. Years later, I interviewed him
on my local TV show (*The Desha Show*) to learn how someone
with so many interests and talents holds it all together.

Daniel is a fine example of someone who is perfectly multi-
passionate—a character, we might say. Refreshing, fun, and
always a bit unexpected. That is Daniel.

Tell me a bit about you . . .
I am a huge Desha Peacock fan! I have lived in and around
Brattleboro, Vermont, for eighteen years. I just bought a 1790s
house with some amazing barns, which I am in the process
of turning into an artist's residency/community arts and
resource center.

This is the first house I've owned. Though it has been well-maintained and is indisputably beautiful, at first I really didn't see myself in it; I always saw myself in something a lot funkier. But once I moved in and tore into it, the dialogue between the space and my ideas began to flow.

As a multi-passionate creative, how does your space influence or contribute to these passions?

I love to be social and I love to work on my art and other projects. I finally have the space that inspires me to continue to be unfettered in my artistic creations and I can host and cook and celebrate with my friends.

How does your home creatively reflect your lifestyle, values, and what's important to you?

I would still like to have more "wild" parts of my living environment—my studio, for example, and perhaps my office. When you walk into my house you can see that I love beauty and to share my space with guests as a place to exchange ideas, support one another, and foster creativity.

What inspires you?

I find inspiration in so many random places. The way the light shines through my curtains, for example, it looks like two strange aliens kissing; a conversation with a random person on the street often sets my mind and spirit buzzing; mishearing lyrics on the radio is a constant source of musical inspiration and, of course, my dreams. Most of my creativity—whether it be a song, a play, or a work of visual art—usually comes to me while I'm sleeping. Needless to say, I need a comfy bed and a dark room.

How does your home reflect your dreams, aspirations, and desires?

A big of part of what makes my home inspirational is landscape. I have huge ancient barns and lots and lots of light. I reside in a bucolic valley with hills, pastures, streams, and trees all around. I have the structures to create a space where artists can come and get things done in an environment that is stimulating and rustic and, ultimately, not that far off a major highway and only hours from two major east coast cities.

Do you have a favorite place in your home that makes you feel like you are thriving in your Sweet Spot?

I have an amazing bedroom (on the blueprints it's referred to as the "borning room") but my kitchen is by far the heart and soul of the house.

What tips do you have to help readers create their own Sweet Spot home on a budget?

Be patient but never lose sight of your vision. I am lucky, I see a space complete after spending some time in it, and then it's just a matter of finding or manifesting the various elements.

Kenny and Chris may have a small space inside, but they have learned to maximize the outdoor space for full on Sweet Spot Living!

small, but mighty

Kenny Osehan: Co-owner of Ojai Rancho Inn and SamaSama Kitchen
Lives in: Santa Barbara, California
Describes her Style as: Organic. Hippie. Modern.

"I never aspired or dreamed of having a home because I never thought it would be possible. My home makes me realize what a great team Chris and I make . . . that the things I never thought possible become reality when Chris and I work together as a team. It's become the perfect canvas for us to feel creatively free."

—Kenny Osehan

Kenny Osehan and hubby Chris Sewell are both passionate when it comes to design. They've blended their unique styles into their seven hundred-square-foot home in a way that creatively reflects their taste and values. Although they manage multiple businesses together, they've still found time to create the home of their dreams within a budget they can afford.

Tell me a bit about you . . .

I live in Santa Barbara with my husband and business partner Chris Sewell. We developed Shelter Social Club to serve as an umbrella for properties we have renovated and rebranded. We own and operate the Ojai Rancho Inn and we are partners with my cousin in an Indonesian inspired restaurant in Santa Barbara called SamaSama Kitchen.

Your story may be a bit different from some women in that it seems your hubby is really into home design as well. Is this true?

Yes, he is more into it than I am actually ... you should probably interview him! He is pretty obsessed with design in general, always researching and scheming about new home projects secretly so I don't get on his case about spending too much money. I'm lucky that he cares about our home so much though, and that he has an amazing aesthetic. He really inspires me in his design perspective.

Kenny and Chris combine their personal tastes to form an aesthetic that is modern, playful, and warm.

How do you create a Sweet Spot home that appeals to you both?
When we met, I really didn't have much of a sense of design. I knew I liked textiles and color and things that looked and felt eccentric. I definitely had a hippie tapestry thing going on. He was really minimalist and his place consisted of a lot of '60s and '70s furniture. As we grew more into our own individual styles, we were able to refine our surroundings in a way that worked well together.

Chris got more into mid-century design and I developed my love of rugs and textiles. Now our styles are much more in line with each other. We have a passion for the organic and wabi-sabi textures of wood and ceramics, especially pieces made by people we know or have become friends with through the love of their work. We mix these pieces in with some mid-century

pieces, *a lot* of textiles and colors, things we find on our travels, add a touch of playfulness . . . and that's how we create our Sweet Spot.

How does your home reflect your values, lifestyle, and what's important to you?

Our home is small but mighty—only seven hundred square feet, but it's perfect for us. It's all about quality over quantity, plus there's less to clean. Chris looked for a home for us every day for four years. This was the first and only home we ever put an offer on. We knew when Chris hopped the fence and opened the door to let me in that this had to be our home.

The most important attribute for our home was that it had to have some sort of architectural significance. This was the biggest challenge because anything that seemed the slightest bit interesting was way over our budget. This is why it took Chris four years of looking until we actually found something we wanted to offer on.

The home was built in 1954 so it is mid-century and has a wall of glass paneling. There is a patio that runs from the front of the house to the side and the backyard has a lot of space and potential. The weather is so mild here that indoor/outdoor living is pretty essential. We like to feel like we are outdoors even when we are inside and the outdoor space is a great extension of our indoor space.

We had our bathroom remodeled so we have a glass door that opens to the backyard from our walk-in shower. We were initially going to put a claw-foot bathtub in, but realized our bathroom was too small and it wouldn't be convenient for everyday showering. The bathtub sat in our backyard for months until I finally convinced Chris to have a deck built outside and run plumbing over to install the bathtub. He was trying to hold out for a hot tub, but when he realized it would be really expensive, he gave in to the outdoor bathtub and now we both really love it. We wanted our home to feel like an escape and a place where we can truly relax. This addition definitely helped us reach that goal.

Community is important to us so we wanted to have a space we could entertain friends. The entire property is very open so it's the perfect place to do just that. We had a friend of ours build a communal table that complements the size and shape of our side patio so it's great for hosting dinner parties. The house is in a great location so it makes you want to go on walks all the time. We are a fifteen minute walk to the ocean, and there's a beautiful park that looks over the entire city that's very close by. We also like to walk or ride bikes into town as much as possible.

We like having our privacy since we are always so social with our line of work. I don't want to go outside and see neighbors all the time. We were lucky that the previous owner's mom was a landscape designer so she designed the fence in a way that provides optimal views and optimal privacy. We are also surrounded by bamboo, tall trees, and plants so we can't really see other homes or the road from anywhere inside or outside our home.

How have you created the space you love on a budget you can afford?

The best advice we got when we moved into our home was to not make any changes until we had lived there for at least a year. This made us really think about how the space flowed and how we lived in it. It made us realize that you shouldn't change anything in your home until you are sure that it's exactly what you want in the price range you can afford. Waiting makes you develop a sense of appreciation for things you didn't think you really liked when you first moved in.

For example, there is a built-in entertainment area that we thought we wanted to get rid of right away, but now that we are living in the space, we realize it's the perfect place for our record player, our books, and our tchotchkes. We'd eventually like to have a fireplace there, but we haven't figured out the right design for that yet. Plus where would we put our tchotchkes? Really giving yourself time instead of diving into renovations is a good way to be sure you are doing exactly what you want to your home without wasting money.

What's one thing that makes your heart sing?

When I open the door into my house and it feels so good that I can't believe it's mine.

How does your home reflect your dreams, aspirations, and desires?

I never aspired or dreamed of having a home because I never thought it would be possible. My home makes me realize what a great team Chris and I make . . . that the things I never thought possible become reality when Chris and I work together as a team. It's become the perfect canvas for us to feel creatively free.

Do you have a favorite place in you home that makes you feel like you are thriving in your Sweet Spot?

When I'm taking a bath outside.

What tips do you have to help others create their own Sweet Spot home?

Be true to what you love.

Headed to Santa Barbara? Stay in Kenny and Chris's Ojai Rancho Inn (ojairanchoinn.com) and grab a bite at SamaSama Kitchen. Yummy!

orchard cabin retreat

Nancy Neil: Professional Photographer and Mother
Lives in: Carpinteria, California
Describes her Style as: Thrift. Gift. Love.

"I know I've chosen the right space to live in when I'm thoroughly excited to be home."

—Nancy Neil

I'm a huge fan of Nancy Neil. She is a sought after photographer whose work has appeared in such prestigious publications as *Elle, Vogue, Glamour, Martha Stewart, Architectural Digest* and many more. Although Nancy travels across the globe for her work, her favorite spot is at home in her cabin retreat surrounded by her children in the quite wooded orchard of Carpinteria.

Tell me a bit about you . . .
I live on an eighty-acre tropical fruit orchard in Carpinteria, CA. It's an old property owned by the same family since 1846. I'm a photographer as well as the mother of two handsome and wild boys.

As a sought after photographer, you've shot loads of gorgeous homes and fashion spreads. How has your work influenced your own personal style?
It's interesting seeing all the different ways people choose to decorate and live in their spaces. In my work, I'm inspired daily by an assortment of designs and also

comforts of the home. Our own home is basically a collection of treasures that embrace us. Cozy, lived-in, and welcoming.

You also have two small children. How do manage to juggle it all and thrive in your work/home?

The only way to survive two busy boys and work as much as I do is first of all you *must* love what you do and second, create a space which embraces the life you have flowing through your home. Every room in the house has a nook or corner that holds the children's things, so each room feels just as much a part of them as me. We share everything—I make messes just as often as they do. Baskets are my favorite for organizing and hiding the clutter that comes along with kids. They can fill them up, dump them out, drag them around—even hide in them. Plus, there are some beautiful functional baskets available.

How does your home reflect your values, lifestyle, and what's important to you?

What's important to me is the connection between myself, my babies, and our "tribe." So most of the "stuff" in our home was a gift or has a great story attached to how it made it's way to our home. There is a significant difference between a house and a home. I want all who enter to feel as though everything belongs to them so they can be themselves, relax, and enjoy each other's company.

What inspires you?

I'm inspired by everything—by color, shape, texture, and how light works with these elements to create a mood. My inspiration changes as often as the light itself!

How does your home reflect your dreams, aspirations, and desires?

My dream was always to live in a secluded open space without all the noise and frills of the city. We can always visit the city! Somehow we managed to find this special space in which to live and grow together. The older parts of the house are my favorite. I love the massive railroad ties that construct the

cabin. They create a warm and protective shelter, which insulates our dreamy mellow lifestyle.

How does your home make you feel like you are thriving in your Sweet Spot?

I know I've chosen the right space to live in when I'm thoroughly excited to be home. I want to spend as much time in this Sweet Spot as possible. It feels like home in more than just the literal sense.

a little breathing room

Kristen James: Interior Stylist, Mom
Derek James: Musician, DJ, Dad
Live in: Laurel Canyon (Los Angeles, California)
Describe their Style as: Tactile. Timeless. Functional.

"The things that are absent from our home definitely reflect a lifestyle we choose to live."

—Kristen James

Kristin and Derek James live in a cozy 1946 cabin right in the middle of one of the biggest, most bustling cities: Los Angeles, California. They lucked out with this cabin in the woods in Laurel Canyon that looks like it could be in the heart of the Ozark Mountains, yet is accessible to big city and creative life, important for a designer and musician. Kristin is a freelance designer and has worked with big names such as Kelly Wearstler and Commune Design. Derek is a musician in the band The Entrance, as well as a DJ. They are proud parents to their darling one-year-old son, Jackson.

Tell me a bit about you . . .

K: I'm an interior designer. I've spent close to fifteen years working on primarily commercial and hotel jobs, but as of this year I'm now working for myself and focusing on smaller projects and hopefully some product collaborations with friends.

D: I'm a musician and DJ.

Derek custom built the shelves and sliding ladder system that leads to a secret nook at the top where you'll find a cozy bedroom for guests or others who want to hideaway.

You live in a cabin surrounded by the woods in L.A. How in the world did you manage that?

Living in beautiful spaces has always been important to both of us and somehow or another we've managed to manifest lots of dream homes over the years. At this point in our lives we've realized that we'd both suffer from the "grass is greener complex" if we had to pick city or country. We love Los Angeles dearly and plan to live here indefinitely, but it has its challenges. So having this cabin tucked away from all the chaos of the city is a huge part of our sanity. Our house is one of two properties that are considered Wildlife Corridor, which means that there is no fencing around our lot and the wildlife (such as deer and coyote) can access our land. Living in close proximity to the mountains, trees, and wildlife is a gift. Our house provides us with a little breathing room (not to mention peace and quiet) from all of the overwhelming elements of the city.

How do your creative passions play into your home decor? Do you guys both have input on the design of your home and if not, how do you manage that?

We absolutely both have input on the design of our house. We're both very opinionated but almost always on the same page aesthetically. We are also

of the same mindset that space evolves and grows and should be filled with treasures and objects you acquire along your journey in life. Very few areas of our home were "designed." Each room is literally a display of our favorite pieces we've collected over the years. Derek's love of music is present in every single room. There are record players and records everywhere! It fills the home with another layer of life and energy that is less visual but equally important to the perception and feel of being in our home. Kristin's obsession for things that are old and handcrafted lends a timelessness to the house that feels comfortable and inviting.

How does your home reflect your values, lifestyle, and what's important to you?

The things that are absent from our home definitely reflect a lifestyle we choose to live. We don't have a dishwasher, microwave, TV, or many modern gadgets. Not that we're living in the dark ages—we are dependent on our computers and cell phones for work and day to day living, but overall we're

Derek found this Rock-Ola jukebox on Ebay. It plays a hand selected mix from the couple's 45 record collection.

low maintenance and enjoy the old way of doing things. We love to cook, entertain, listen to records, build fires, read our books, and our house is set up to do all of those things really well!

What inspires you?
We're inspired by anything done by someone who cares about what they're creating. There's tons of beauty in honed craft, skill, mistakes, imperfection, perfection.

How does your home make you feel like you are thriving in your Sweet Spot?
Every time we return to our house after traveling we realize we've become so completely dialed in to our space. The quiet neighborhood, the beautiful light that changes all year long, the plants and animals . . . it's all wonderful. The kitchen is also a big deal. We cook a lot at home and it's really hard to be somewhere when that's not an option.

What tips do you have to help others create their own Sweet Spot home on a budget? Examples?
Stay away from the big chain stores that are constantly reinventing home trends (and overflowing landfills). Save up and/or hold out for things you love! Never underestimate the treasure to be found on eBay, Craigslist, garage sales, and thrift stores. Craigslist in particular is amazing. There are people selling anything and everything.

Notice how Kristin and Derek use rugs to help separate dining, lounging, and conversation spaces—a helpful technique to make a large room feel cozy.

Finding value in the process

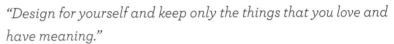

Kelly Bone: Commercial Interior Designer, Food Writer

Lives in: Los Angeles, California

Describes her Style as: Wood. Patterns. Details.

"Design for yourself and keep only the things that you love and have meaning."

—Kelly Bone

Food writer and commercial interior designer Kelly Bone found clarity in moving cross-country. A hoarder at heart, she was forced to address the value and meaning of her material objects in the move, a process that allowed her to consider what's truly important in her life.

Tell me a bit about you . . .
You know the cubicles you or your friends sit in? I'm the one who designs them. I work in the commercial interior design field and it's totally different from residential. In fact, I've intentionally avoided residential design because it is so emotionally driven—but I can't avoid designing my own home.

It's a personal process. Even when people feel their home has no order or meaning, that in and of itself is a design choice. We choose who and what we surround ourselves with and we have to deal with ourselves in the process.

That sounds dire . . . ultimately it is a fun process, a chance for self-exploration and creativity.

Other than that, for the past two and a half years I've also been a food writer focusing on pizza in Los Angeles. A lot of people claim to have eaten bad pizza in LA, to which I ask: Why did you go to a place that served bad pizza? In the same way, a lot of people claim to lack the skill or money to design their home. But did they not choose to have or keep everything within it? Whatever is important in life to you, be it good pizza or a comfortable home, it's up to you to make it. Home and pizza just happen to be what I do.

How does your home reflect who you are and your lifestyle?
I spent my 20s living in New York City. Moving cross-country forced me to take stock of my belongings, sifting through a decade of life. My LA apartment is now a hodge-podge of a new and old existence. At first I thought about throwing it all away; but minimalism proved more expensive than I thought. There is value in bits and bob of ribbon, a square of wrapping paper, a tube of super glue, or a box of assorted nails. Life is eased by having these things at hand.

Moving made me consider every object, assessing intrinsic value on material items, passing judgment on which memories were worth taking with me. There are a few simple things I wish I'd kept: A slotted spoon I thought would be easy to replace or a $2 wooden spice rack I never considered unique. I miss these things. But my home now reflects a happy medium between two coasts, compromises I've made with myself and the improvements to my state. I should probably explain that I'm a bit of a hoarder. But I've whittled my material possessions down to the essentials and found some clarity in the process. It just so happens that piles of Sassy and Colors magazines and a white enamel stand mixer are, in my mind, essentials.

My grandmother is also a big-time hoarder and I can feel the impulse within me. I over-sentimentalize objects and feel a loss at their disappearance, such as that slotted spoon. I try to be rational, only holding on to an item that evokes memories; knowing that otherwise it's just junk. When I left that spoon behind, I assumed I'd find the

same or better in California. I haven't . . . yet. Sometimes simple things take longer than expected. Or maybe I should just go buy a spoon.

You described your apartment as "budget rad." What are some examples of how you've created the space you love on a budget you can afford?

Refinished furniture is my preferred method for creating unique personal items. For example, a neighbor in Brooklyn left behind two wooden side chairs. Half stripped, with hideous torn up vinyl upholstery, the well-constructed bones of these handcrafted wooden chairs was too obvious to discard. I used them as-is for years. Once I had the time and money to sponsor their restoration, I found a local upholsterer with reasonable prices and a modern selection of fabrics. Thrift stores and flea market finds fill out the rest of my apartment.

How does your home reflect your values and what's important to you?

Life is complicated. A home is one of the few parts of life you have control over. Every day I trip through the outside world; when I come home I don't want to trip over my belongings. A lot of what surrounds me are gifts from my family. There are touches of my mother everywhere—her used casserole dishes, a coffee table we carried through a flea market together, the carpet pad that keeps my bathroom rug from slipping all over the place. When I moved from NYC, my parents filled the holes in my home.

How does your home reflect *you*, your dreams, aspirations, and desires?

Dreams, aspirations, and desires speak towards the future. At this point I'm catching up to the present. What I see in my home is a curated display of my past, taken from moments I wish to remember. Not all are pleasant. Trinkets from friendships gone sour reside in plain sight, a reminder to be good to those who love you in the present. But so much of it is grand. My fruit bowl

held sweets at my best friend's wedding, a plastic white cat pencil sharpener was a "just because" gift from another dear friend.

When apartment hunting I looked for kitchens with room to expand, flowing into the dining and living room. I knew I wouldn't be able to afford the kitchen I wanted; instead I looked for the potential in a space. My father is a carpenter. He built out a counter with cabinets into the dining room, turning the ridiculously designed apartment kitchen into a usable space. So much of my house wears the fingerprints of my parents.

Do you have a favorite place in you home that makes you feel like you are thriving in your Sweet Spot?
It used to be the kitchen but, ironically, since I began food writing I rarely cook. These days, my Sweet Spot is in my bed. It offers a sky view through my bedroom window. I often lie there, two grey cats curled up by my side, and consider the future.

What tips do you have to help others create their own Sweet Spot home?
Design for yourself and keep only the things that you love and have meaning. If I don't connect with an item, out it goes . . . or so I try to tell myself.

Find out how not to eat bad pizza on Kelly's food blog, thevegetarianfoodie.com.

Kelly and her grandmother, who taught her to follow her own taste.

community, food & art

Corri Bristow Sundell: Mother, Artist, Co-Owner of The Root (Café)
Lives in: Little Rock, Arkansas
Describes her Style as: Homegrown. Eclectic. Organized.

"The world is full of wonder and beauty. I love gathering inspiration, bringing it home, doing what I can to try and make things better."

—Corri Bristow

Let's just be clear, this is my best friend from Arkansas and I love her dearly! Now that that's out of the way, Corri is not only inspirational with how she sets up her home, but also her life. A big influence in my life, Corri knows how to create the coziest home, always full of food, family and friends—all the things that are important to her and make us feel right at home. And that's why we love her!

Tell me a bit about you . . .

I am an Arkansas gal and a southern mama. I'm happily married to my life's love, Jack, who is also my business partner, and I'm the mother of a fantastic, charismatic, talented young man. We have two dogs, two cats, two chickens, and we all live together in our 1920s Arts and Crafts bungalow, typical of our mid-town Little Rock neighborhood, Stifft Station. Actually, the hens live in a

scrap-wood lean-to, added to our shed in 2008. We're also expecting twin boys!

I grew up here in Arkansas and I appreciate the closeness of community and deepness of kinships that slow living allows. I like to travel, too. The world is full of wonder and beauty. I love gathering inspiration, bringing it home, doing what I can to try and make things better.

My husband and I opened our dream business in 2011 after three years of saving and planning. It's a little local-foods restaurant called The Root Café in the heart of the SOMA (South Main) neighborhood of Little Rock's downtown historic district. Our mission is "Building Community through Local Food," and we're doing our best to live up to it. We source absolutely as much as we can from small farms and small distributors here in Arkansas, which has

turned out to be just about everything. We're a made-from-scratch, small-batch kind of place. We host community events and often work cooperatively with other businesses and neighbors to help bring folks together.

Before we opened the café, I worked as an artist. I worked mostly in editorial illustration and, for a spell, in historic restoration. I also spent a lot of time doing community-action work. All of it was fabulous, fulfilling work for me, and folks sometimes ask how I relieve that creative itch. That is, now that my former art studio is my Root office space. To me, what I'm doing now is the perfect marriage of my life's passions: building community and creativity.

I also really enjoy being home and sitting around with the ones I love, playing music, drinking coffee (or

tea), swapping stories over, dare I say it, shelling peas . . . or often pecans, depending on the season.

You are a mother, artist, and co-owner of The Root. How does your home reflect your lifestyle, values, and what's important to you?
Although my dear husband mostly gives me creative control over the aesthetics of our home, it is a reflection of the things that mean the most to us as a family. It's a place where we all love to be. With me being a visual artist, and my husband a musician, we surround ourselves in a community of creative-type folks. Our home is certainly a reflection of that. It is filled with original arts and crafts made by artists whom we know and adore.

Jack's grandfather was a fantastic artist, and we've been lucky to be able to include several of his works in our collection. Alongside the art, we often hang musical instruments, some still in use and some retired. And in handmade bowls are fresh fruit and vegetables, harvested by farmer friends. Beautiful and delicious!

Our furniture is a mix-match of family antiques, junk store finds, and even the occasional roadside treasure. From our travels, we've collected and now display keepsakes and trinkets that trigger fond memories and inspire new projects and ideas. Jack's dad, a retired botanist, helps us to appreciate the beauty of the outdoors, and we often display samplings of dried leaves and plant pods, which keep the beauty of nature alive in our minds.

How have you created the space you love on a budget you can afford? Can you give some examples?

I come from a family of junk collectors. My dad has always been an antique lover, and since his retirement about ten years ago, he's been able to focus on that passion full-time. That is, trading antiques. He loves anything old that comes with or inspires a good story. He's also really good at pinching pennies and has done his best to teach me the value of simple living, making the most of what I have, and keeping within my means. So, I guess I just try to do what I can with what I have.

For example, the tiles of our kitchen backsplash were very run-of-the-mill, box-store home-improvement type. I didn't want to go through the trouble or the expense of replacing them, but I sure didn't love them! Also, the pulls on my kitchen cabinets were very contemporary, swirly-style brushed nickel pulls. Fine, but not my style.

The tiles were a checkerboard pattern of navy and burnt-orange faux-stone and held together with pale-gray grout. I got my hands on some glass and ceramic paints, grout, and concrete stain. I stained the grout a dark brown, painted the tiles different shades of creamy white and earthy orange tones, and then I stenciled them with stencils that I bought, cut myself, and collected during my time in historic restoration. Some of the flowers stenciled on my kitchen tiles, albeit different in color, can also be found in the frieze of the apse of a historic cathedral here in town! Last, I covered the tiles with a brush-on, clear ceramic topcoat to give them a nice sheen and bring it all together.

For my cabinet and drawer pulls, I looked and looked for ones that

were simple and affordable. I looked in junk shops, but I needed twenty-five! I looked online and in decorators' shops, but they were so expensive. Finally, I looked in my favorite neighborhood hardware store, and there they were. Old-fashioned, cream-colored ceramic pulls. They're the type with a dull, brass screw in the middle. They were less than $2 for two in a pack. They had all that I needed in stock. What a find!

What's one thing that makes your heart sing?

I love to allow myself the time to find just the right thing at just the right price. For example, I have this old brass lamp. For a long time, it had a ragtag lampshade that wasn't really the right size or style or color. I looked here and there when I was out and about. Sometimes I might see one for the right price, but it just wouldn't be the right shade. Other times, I might see a shade that would do, but then the price would be more than I would want to spend. Then, one day at junk shop, there it was. I loved the size, shape, and style. It was perfect. It was $1. And my heart did sing.

Do you have a favorite place in you home that makes you feel like you are thriving in your Sweet Spot?

That's a hard one to answer. I suppose I try and create that feeling in every part of our home, including the outside spaces like the porch and the yard. We have a lovely wrought-iron swing in our front yard that sits under the giant sycamore tree that shades almost our entire house. I love to sit there and look

"We've created a space that inspires us and reminds us of what we love."

out over my yard of mostly shade-loving plants, including a lot of ferns in found pots, and visit with friends and neighbors who pass by on afternoon walks. That's a pretty sweet spot to remind me of my Sweet Spot. I also love every room in my house. I swear I do! We've created a space that inspires us and reminds us of what we love.

What tips do you have to help others create their own Sweet Spot home?

You don't have to spend big to create a space that you love. At least, that's what I've found to be true. I can work with what I have. I can do a lot myself. I can love what I have. And with patience, I can wait for just the right thing. It's always worth it.

You've got to check out Little Rock and when you do, stop in at The Root Café and give Corri a big hug from her dear old friend. therootcafe.com

multi passionate creative explorer

Erin Lorenzen: Artist, Fashion Designer, Yoga Teacher
Lives in: Little Rock, Arkansas
Describes her Style as: Eclectic. Exotic. Down-Home.

"I have one large white wall in the center of my studio. I feel like anything is possible in front of that big white wall."

—Erin Lorenzen

Fashion designer, artist, and yoga teacher, Erin Lorenzen blends work and play in her home studio located at the Kramer School, situated in the historic urban area of downtown Little Rock, Arkansas.

As a multi-passionate creative, how does your space influence or contribute to these passions?
This is the perfect space for me. It's on the corner of the building and has two full walls of tall windows, awesome light, high ceilings, and wide-open space. It is filled with objects from my family, friends, travels, art supplies, inspiration sketches, quotes, photographs, and color. I love color. It makes me happy. Being surrounded by all of these things reminds me of the endless possibilities there are in life. Being in this space reminds me of my favorite travel spots: India, Morocco, Mexico, and South America. It reminds me not to take things so seriously. It inspires me to continue to explore, push boundaries, invent, and create.

My home is my a nest, a hive, a safe, sacred space where I feel like it's okay to do whatever I want, to create whatever I want, and not worry what other people think about it. In this space I get to make art for arts sake, for the sake of exploration, for the sake of fun.

What's life like in Little Rock, AR?

Quiet. Little Rock is a wonderful home base. The people are friendly, there is a quickly growing healthy community of yogis, cyclists, runners, and climbers. There are great restaurants and a thriving music scene. The cost of living is also super reasonable and allows for lots of travel. This is one of my favorite things. I love a new frontier.

Tell me about the Kramer School and what it's like living there as a creative.

Although no longer officially an artist co-op, the building still serves as low income housing, which continues to attract starving artists like yours truly. It was built in 1895 for only $11,000 and named after Frederick Kramer, a civic leader and former mayor of Little Rock. It's an awesome building with perfect space and light for making art. And this neighborhood in general is attracting more and more creative people.

I feel like downtown Little Rock is finally starting to "happen." The River Market makeover continues, but the Creative Corridor project is bringing everything from the River Market to SOMA (historic urban neighborhood of Southside Main Street) to life bit by bit. I think it won't be too long until the entire area is full of artists and creative types. I think LR is an awesome place for artists right now.

How does your home reflect your dreams, inspirations, and desires?

I basically live inside my sketchbook. I used to always carry a small one with me. I usually kept it bound, tied up, so the things I stuffed in there wouldn't fall out. Bit by bit, I started putting sketches on the wall before I started working on a project. And gradually, it just turned into a whole big pinboard. Now, I'm completely surrounded by sketches, clippings, and photos. It helps me remember all of the amazing things that inspire me and all of the things I want to do in life all of the time rather than just when I open up my little sketchbook.

"You can create whatever you want with your surroundings." —Erin

Do you have a favorite place in your home that makes you feel like you are thriving in your Sweet Spot?

The big white wall. I kind of have a lot going on, so I try to focus on only one big project at a time. I have one large white wall in the center of my studio. I feel like anything is possible in front of that big white wall.

Like most artists who work in color, Erin needs some white space in her life to gain clarity around new projects. She uses the large, open, white wall to the left as a blank canvas to explore and generate new ideas. She says, "It's like one big pin board."

What tips do you have to help readers create their own Sweet Spot on a Home Budget?

Everything in this place is made from hand-me-downs, scraps, and straight up trash. Repainting and repurposing can do wonders. You can always find mis-mixed paint at paint stores for a discounted price. You can repair damaged pieces of furniture others are throwing out. Just look at everything around you as a blank canvas. You can create whatever you want with your surroundings.

Check out Erin's Etsy shop online and get me an "I love AR" shirt while you're there (wink, wink)! etsy.com/shop/shopELL

jungalow love

Justina Blakeney: Mother, Creative Consultant, Curator, Stylist, Author
Lives in: Los Angeles, California
Describes her Style as: Jungalicious.Globoh (global/bohemian), Creative.

"When you make space for things you want in your home and in your life, those things have an easier time coming into your life."

—Justina Blakeney

Justina Blakeney is a fine example of a multi-passionate creative who has managed to combine many of her passions and interests into a successful career, while also staying home with her young daughter, Ida. Justina combines her love for interior styling, home design, photography, and art into her popular lifestyle blog and creative projects. With four books under her belt and over one million Pinterest followers, her global, bohemian style, approachable voice, and *jungalow* inspire people all over the world to get wild with their home decor.

Her daily lifestyle blog, *Justina Blakeney Est. 1979*, was recently named one of the Best Decor Blogs by *Refinery 29*. *Martha Stewart Weddings* calls her a "creative tour de force" while Apartment Therapy hails her a "creative genius." *Dwell* magazine named Justina's Pinteriors board a top 10 design board on Pinterest while editors over at Design Sponge are "longtime fans of Justina Blakeney's style."

Tell me a bit about you . . .

Even as a child I was very art and design oriented. I loved to paint, sew, and create collages. After studying art in college I moved to Italy and began to think about design as a way to make a living using my creative talents. I opened a small boutique for vintage and new designer clothing and I found that after a few years, I was most excited about the act of finding vintage objects and furniture for the shop. That's when I realized my deep passion for décor and began working on home décor projects. I originally began blogging as a way to do something creative everyday. I loved blogging right away as it was a natural way to combine so many of the things that I love including writing, photography, graphic design, crafting, styling, collaging, curating, and decorating.

I live in my plantastic Jungalow on the east side of Los Angeles with my husband Jason, our daughter Ida, and cat Luda. I was raised in Berkeley,

California but lived abroad in Switzerland for two years as a teenager, and then spent seven years in Florence, Italy in my twenties.

People hire me as a creative consultant. That can mean anything from decorating and styling to art directing, shopping, and branding. Sometimes I get paid to craft pretty stuff out of crazy materials or to curate art works and wares, which is pretty great, too. Basically, if it's creative, fun, and fresh, chances are, I'm down to work on it! I'm pretty nerdy so I geek out a lot with graphics, but the hands-on stuff is what I find the most fun. Now, my blog is also a source of income for me so I suppose you could say I'm a pro-blogger, too.

You are a creative consultant, curator, stylist, and author. When I look at your blog I am mostly inspired, but I have to admit I'm a little bit jealous, too. Is this your dream work?
Honestly, when I was a kid I wanted to be a singer. That was my dream. But now, as an adult, I wouldn't want to be doing anything else!

As a multi-passionate creative and mother how do you manage to juggle it all and thrive in your work and home?
I do it with a lot of help! My husband and I both work from home so we take turns taking care of Ida. Included in our schedule is a dedicated time for the three of us to be together, which is really important to our family. Honestly, lots of things fall through the cracks, but ultimately the vital stuff gets done, even if the house is often messy or the plants don't get watered every once in awhile.

How does your home reflect your values, lifestyle, and what's important to you?
My home is a bright, multi-culti amalgamation of mostly old and handmade items from my travels and DIY projects of the last ten or so years. My home is certainly a multi-functional space that sometimes acts as a nursery, an office, a boutique,

a restaurant, an office—you name it! My home reflects my lifestyle and values because I, too, am all over the place and I, too, have that dichotomy of being an "old soul" but also being, at times, hyper-modern, a little tattered around the edges, creative, and colorful. Our house is pretty green—we compost, have solar panels on our roof, we get all of our produce from our CSA box, we have a modest garden that we eat from when possible. Most everything in the home (furniture, art, etc.) was purchased secondhand. This is very important to my husband and me and I'm proud of it. We are working towards being even more sustainable.

What inspires you?
My mother is a huge inspiration to me. She handles everything so gracefully and in such a humble way. She's also the smartest person that I know. I admire Frida Kahlo, Josephine Baker, Bjork, Jonathan Adler, Audrey Hepburn. I'm

also inspired so much by people who are skilled craftspeople and who have a great eye and a unique perspective. And as far as aesthetic inspiration goes, traveling, plants and flowers, and vintage textiles inspire me.

How does your home reflect your dreams, aspirations, and desires?
I suppose that I dreamt of having a family, and Jason and I moved from a one-bedroom into a two bedroom and sure enough a year later I got pregnant. I think when you make space for things you want in your home and in your life, those things have an easier time coming into your life.

Do you have a favorite place in your home that makes you feel like you are thriving in your Sweet Spot?

I love to sit in the corner of the couch by the two windows in my living room. It's very lounge-y, the lighting is soft and romantic, and the windows provide a nice breeze. It's my little cozy and creative nook where I write my blog, sip on coffee, and brainstorm kooky new schemes.

What tips do you have to help others create their own Sweet Spot home on a budget?

Let it be cozy, let it have nice natural light, let there be fresh air, a few plants, a few of your favorite things.

Check out Justina's colorious blog @ justinablakeney.com and look for her new book in 2015 tentatively titled *The New Bohemian*.

JUSTINA'S SWEET SPOT TIPS

- It's amazing what a few potted plants will do to increase your quality of life.
- If you're sick of your furniture, try painting it a bright, outlandish color: turquoise, fuchsia, kelly green . . . it's mind-blowing how color can punctuate a space.
- Change the light fixtures in your home—even in a rental—it's one of those things that makes a *huge* difference and doesn't have to be expensive.

social consciousness and freedom

Susie Belleci: Global Conflict Transformation Instructor, Mother, Wife
Lives in: Brattleboro, Vermont
Describes her Style as: Conscious. Soothing. Reaffirming of her Values.

"Don't be defeated. The doors will open. Follow your heart. Follow your values. Follow your beliefs and the doors will open."

—Susie Belleci

International educator and world traveler, Susie Belleci, primarily furnished her house from the Swap Shop (aka: the dump!). Susie's home décor is heavily influenced by her values. All of her furniture and home accessories were either free or under $10. Hers is a great story that appeals to women with a social conscience and interest in environmental sustainability and human rights.

Tell me a bit about you . . .

I am a conflict transformation instructor at the School for International Training and I offer global peace building and training around the world. My husband Lasse is Danish and so, so great! Our amazing son Gabriel is seven. Lasse and I met in Palestine where he was doing human rights work and I was teaching at the American University in Jenin. While in Palestine I saw a lot of suffering, as you can imagine, but I've seen it in many of the places where

I've lived and worked. Those experiences have influenced my lifestyle and ultimately the choices I make around my home.

How has living abroad affected your value system and how is this reflected in your home?

While living for a couple of years on a beautiful tropical island in the Pacific, I observed an American company that came in and built a tee shirt factory. Their intent was to hire locals and give them an opportunity to earn some money. However, after one week everybody quit because the hours were very long and it was very hot with no way to see outside. People lived pretty close to their ancient ways of life on that island with plenty of fish to catch inside the reef and fruits on the trees to eat, so life was relatively easy.

You have to understand that in this culture, people think sending a child to her room is cruel punishment; sending one human being away from another is wrong in their view, and sending them to a closed space where they'd feel trapped is unimaginable. So the locals didn't feel it was worth it to work in this sort of windowless factory, and they quit. Thus, the company had to bring in Filipino workers from off-island. We saw the young women come in, but we didn't see them leave until a year later.

We sometimes observed at a distance and noticed the women weren't allowed outside the factory grounds. I remember thinking, *Here we live in paradise and these women are locked in this factory and sending home money to their families.*

Later, in Washington DC, I participated in a workshop on child labor and sweat shops. I asked, "What can I buy and know that children haven't made it or that young women weren't locked in factories for 14 hours a day to produce it?" The presenter said that unless it's labeled "certified fair trade," there's no way of knowing. This pretty much cuts out all major brands.

In that moment, I decided I did not want to contribute to this kind of human suffering, and to be sure that I wasn't, I would not buy anything new. I couldn't stop the whole system, but I could at least control my own buying habits and make sure that I didn't personally contribute to what I consider to be slave labor.

It wasn't too much of a problem until I became pregnant and my family was *so* excited and wanted to throw me a huge Italian American baby shower and buy me lots and lots of new clothes for the baby.

I had to decide: Am I going to impose this lifestyle on my child, too? When I thought about dressing my baby in a brand new outfit from Macy's that might have been made from a woman who hasn't seen her own baby in months, maybe years, I just couldn't bear it. I had to tell my mother either used items, or no shower.

It caused an uproar in my family, but it was clear to me that I couldn't sleep if I consented to these purchases on my behalf. Luckily, my husband was on board.

How does your home reflect who you are and your lifestyle?

When we bought our home, I had to put living these values to the ultimate test because we simply didn't own *anything*. I was forty-five years old, and all these years living overseas in furnished homes we never had to buy this stuff. We didn't own dishes, a mop, broom, towels, lawnmower or anything and we spent all our money on buying the house, so there wasn't anything extra.

The night we first moved into our house I cried and cried. I'd lived in these charming, historic houses around the world, yet our first home was wall to wall fake veneer paneling, fake linoleum floors, ugly light fixtures . . . every room was despairing for me because I didn't know how to make it beautiful in a way that would align with my values and budget. I felt totally trapped by my values and yet I felt I couldn't abandon them.

The first miracle came when my son made best friends with the wonderful boy next door. That was a dream come true. The hours they spent together in our house, their house, and our shared backyard gave me time, which gave me freedom.

I discovered the Swap Shop (aka the dump!) where everything is free. The first thing we needed was chairs and a table. My husband Lasse was a case manager for at-risk youth during the day and at night wanted to be with our son as much as possible, so he didn't have a lot of time to spend working on projects around the house. I figured if I wanted decent chairs, I'd have to learn out how to make them look good on my own. The chairs at the Swap Shop were layered with various colors of paint and were all different sizes and shapes.

I didn't know how to sand a chair, paint, or even use a hammer! I just told myself, one thing at a time. I got some tips from Lasse, looked on YouTube, and ended up refinishing all six chairs. They didn't cost me anything and I really liked them. I realized I could do this. I could get free things at the Swap Shop and on Free Cycle to decorate my house and I could learn to remodel it by laying tile and wood floors, painting walls, stripping, varnishing, and repairing old pieces of furniture.

Can you tell me about your $10 policy and how this practice reflects your values and what's important to you?

I have a strict policy. I don't want to support slave or child labor and I refuse to go into debt to buy something beyond my budget. So, the system is that most everything I get is free and would otherwise end up in a landfill. However, I will buy something if it is under $10, as long as it is used or certified fair trade. For example, I found these beautiful Kilim pillows in Iraq at the fairly traded crafts market. They were under $10, I knew the source, and I happily bought them.

However, I might see a lovely fair trade linen dress that I want, but if it's $150 I won't buy it because I have other priorities and values to maintain. Staying on a strict home budget has also allowed for one of us to be home with our son while he is young. At one point, we were living on my husband's income of $35,000 a year, yet we were still able to buy a home, furnish it, and continue to eat a one hundred percent organic diet. We didn't spend money on going out to eat or home furnishings. I'm serious when I say this—we didn't even buy a hairdryer or clothes pins. We got almost every single item in our home for free. It was more important for us to have one parent home than to have stuff, so we found ways to make this system work.

On top of that we made a promise to raise our son bi-culturally, and going to Denmark for

A lovely little breakfast nook includes chairs and a bench found for free at the Swap Shop (aka the dump), flowers from the garden, and fresh strawberry scones made by Lasse.

three weeks each year is a huge expense. Because we don't spend money on our home, we are able to travel every single year. It's our choice. You know, everyone has a choice, and this is the one that feels good to us now. Maybe in the future when we are both working, I would choose to buy more expensive fairly traded products. I would love to be able to do that, but I also get a lot of joy and satisfaction from how things are now.

How does your home reflect *you*, your dreams, aspirations, and desires?

Well it's tied to my work. Right now I work with twenty-two peace builders from conflict zones around the world and none of them knows my house is a reflection of my work. I don't bring it up when we talk about child soldiers or the mines in the DRC (Democratic Republic of the Congo) where children risk their lives to get the minerals needed to make computers or cell phones. I don't say, "Well one thing you can do is get used computers." I hesitate to talk about it. I don't want it to sound like I'm bragging and I don't want others to feel I'm judging them. I'm even a little nervous about telling you this now, because I don't want people to read this and say, "Who does she think she is?" Like my loving mother might say, "I *love* going to Macy's and those department stores are full of workers that need jobs." I don't want to get into all that with other people; this is what weaves well with my life and my work and my heart. It sits well with me. I really don't judge other people around this. Many of my family members are huge shoppers and I still love them very much. In fact, I admire the things in their homes. I look around and think, "Hum, how could I do the exact same thing with free things?"

When people compliment my house, I still am not sure if I believe them. I grew up in an affluent family where the price of things was equated with the quality of things and so there's still a part of me that says, "How could you believe that's a beautiful chair . . . I got that for free!" But in my secret moments, when I see the sixty-year-old wooden rolling desk chair that I got for free, but that could easily be mistaken for a $300 chair from Pottery Barn, I feel prosperous and proud.

What's one bit of advice you'd give others who want to create their own Sweet Spot home on a budget?

When I first started decorating this home, I didn't really have an eye for design. I just never noticed these things the way most women seem to early in life. So, I started cutting out magazine pictures of what I did like and visualizing and manifesting it for my house. I got many things just by asking. I asked for a picket fence and I got one free. I asked friends for perennials and they brought them over and told me where to plant them. For several years, I wanted an off white couch with slipcovers. Just recently I traded a gift certificate to a friend for her couch and it's just like the one I had envisioned. It takes time, but you can do it. Just be patient with the process. If someone told me that my house would look like this in just three years with very little money, I wouldn't have believed it. I didn't know I could learn to sand and stain floors, or add doors to an armoire. And the fact that my son magically found a best friend to spend long hours with opened up the time I needed to do the work and hunt for free things. So, I'd say don't be defeated. The doors will open. Follow your heart. Follow your values. Follow your beliefs and the doors will open.

Susie and Lasse's home is full of art by Lasse's father, a famous painter in Denmark. Influenced by his father's eye for texture and paint, Lasse allowed the history of this salvaged door to remain, an indication he has his father's artistic sensibilities when it comes to design.

Much of the book you are reading right now was written right here in this living room during Salon.

the dollhouse

Suzanne Kingsbury: Author, Development Editor, Founder of Wild Words

Lives in: Brattleboro, Vermont

Describes her Style as: Sensual. Classic. Artistic.

"Above all, let your home nurture you, let it hold you, let it be the one place you feel you can do very little wrong."

—Suzanne Kingsbury

One of my dearest friends, literary icon Suzanne Kingsbury, remodeled her 1876 Victorian "dollhouse" to reflect her unique personal style infusing soft whites with rich bohemian textures, creating an effect that is both luxurious and comfy cozy. Originally designed by a priest for his new bride, the home was built on a hill oriented towards the heavens. A beautiful spiral staircase winds its way up to the private tower providing the perfect writer's retreat.

Photographs, a framed marriage certificate, and handwritten love notes add a personal touch reflecting the importance of love and marriage. Suzanne added white silk and velvet textiles to mimic the natural light pouring in from all angles, offering a clean, feminine look.

The living room doubles as a casually elegant hangout for friends and family, and an intimate space for *Salon*, where Suzanne and other writers share a glass of wine, write from the heart, and connect with their own creative Sweet Spots.

Get creative and use a vintage chest of drawers to hold your sink as Suzanne did.

Tell me a bit about you . . .

I am primarily a novelist but am in the midst of writing a how-to memoir on yoga and writing: *Wild Words, Beautiful Body*, with yoga guru Diana Whitney. I am also a book shaman. I help new writers bring their book dreams alive through salon-style retreats and one-on-one editing. The teaching method I use draws from the writer's strengths and instinct, making writing an incredibly fluid, intuitive act. The writer finds herself in a creative space that feels like home and careers are born. I help them connect with agents, get book contracts, and hit the bestseller list.

How does your home creatively reflect your lifestyle, values, and what's important to you?

Our house is an 1800s Victorian built by a minister for his young wife on one of the highest points in Brattleboro, Vermont. You can feel ascension in it, an orientation toward the heavens in the pointed gothic windows and the "tower" that sits on top. The house seems to communicate the sense that a

The spiraling staircase adds intrigue and a bit of mystery as you make your way up and around towards the "tower."

great force is at work in the world. It reflects an almost constant fascination I have with the spiritual. I particularly believe in books as dictums from a higher source, and consider the act of writing an otherworldly undertaking in service to the sacred. Whether the books that haunt us arrive from the ghosts of our ancestry, from past lives, or from a sort of dreamscape from another world, being called to scribe is a divine gift. This feeling of ascension in the architecture, the movement toward that higher place, mirrors that belief beautifully and provides the perfect setting to produce divine writing.

What inspires you?

The walls in our home are painted California Gardenia, a soft white, with Sugar trim. After we had it painted, it occurred to me how much like a blank page the walls are. The space seems to beckon creativity, meditation, and gestation on the imaginative process. We punctuated the white with paintings from artists' friends, beaded silk lampshades that throw moving light on the walls, oriental rugs passed down from my mother's side, masks I bought at market stalls in Africa—all objects infused with meaning. This is a rich metaphor for the way a sheet of paper is punctuated by words that contain power and clarity of meaning. The white space between holds the creative urge.

Views of Brattleboro, Vermont from the Dollhouse.

How does your home reflect your dreams, aspirations, and desires?
My aspirations, dreams, and desires are all about nurturing creative
expression. I mean "nurture" in a very literal sense. Massage, delicious
food, supportive collaboration, warmth, unconditional positive regard—it's
all necessary to call forth the creative. I named the house "The Dollhouse"
because it reminds me of those old dollhouses you see at antique shows.
And because you can always be a child here, you can play. It looks big on the
outside, but inside it's actually quite compact and cozy.

Because of this coziness and its unique architecture—the way the walls slant
and seem to "hold" its occupants—The Dollhouse is the perfect place to be
nurtured as a creative. It's one of the many creative hubs in our little arts'
town. Here we hold the infamous Tuesday night salon and when that gets
too big, one on Thursday mornings, too. I also hold kids' salons after school.

And I work with writers one-on-one here. The salons and the one-on-one work are about splonking the creative soul and teaching writers to lean into their strengths and to let themselves be supported as writers.

The more you nurture yourself, the more your critic takes a backseat and falls asleep. And when the critic is asleep? That's when the genesis of great work is born. Here we have the space to talk about where the writer's talent lives. Once a writer understands this, they burst through creative limitations they didn't know they had. We all feel high in the midst of salon and for a long time afterwards. What happens in The Dollhouse is sacred and largely unexplainable. The house holds it all. Everything—its high ceilings, white velvet couches, feather-pillows, soft lighting and of course the wine and chocolate—seems to say, *it's alright, go ahead, take the leap: Create!*

Do you have a favorite place in your home that makes you feel like you are thriving in your Sweet Spot?

The tower is my Sweet Spot. The four windows give you a view of the four directions. My grandmother's drop leaf oak desk sits against the east wall whose window looks out onto a mountain over the Connecticut River. The desk is around the same age as the house and has seen its share of divorce and death. People have stashed money and love letters in its secret drawer. It was hidden for a long time in a Cape Cod storage shed and the cubbies are falling apart. This imperfection gives the owner permission to be imperfect herself. My grandmother once conducted business from it. She was six feet tall with a pound of ringing bangles on each arm, bright lipstick, and flashing black eyes. She smoked Pall Malls and insisted she had the lungs of a 12 year old. She was a fierce success in business and yet never took it too

Global textures on the bed in the Tower.

seriously. We writers might do the same. We too have to be businesspeople, we must know how to play with marketing, negotiate contracts, court publicity, and yet we don't want to do this at the expense of our art.

For the imaginative child inside, I have hung wood-carved puppets from the walls. My friend Bethanie laughed when she saw the bed up there. Why not be comfortable when we write? It's interesting what happens when you nurture a creative. So I write in that bed and Skype with my writers from there. I also get shiatsu treatments, make love, and sometimes just lie down and listen to the wind blow through the trees.

Writers often sleep over after salon in the tower. Memoirist Katina Makris has slept there, the classical composer Spencer, YA novelist Lava Mueller, and others. I affectionately call the tower, "The Cloud." It's a place where you can float through the world while also doing what you need to survive, whether creatively or otherwise. We've watched fireworks and storms and stars from The Cloud. It's the smallest, most imaginative room in the house and besides the kitchen it's where I spend the most time.

Suzanne's grandmother's dress hangs on the door holding memories and a dash of glamour.

Love notes from Peter casually strewn about the house provide a testament to the passion that fills the home.

What tips do you have to help readers create their own Sweet Spot home on a budget?

Home is unique to each person. Walk into any home and you get a sense of values, of who the person is. Advice is hard because it's almost like treading on someone's soul. For me, I like to get pieces that have lasted through the ages, that will never go out of style. I always rely on the classics: rich wood antiques, beadboard, traditional tile patterns, wide wood floors, vintage brass lamps. I don't really think about following trends. I often have fresh flowers from the gardens and find antique shop frames for photographs of my family and for the love notes my husband leaves me in the morning. I try to buy when I travel so I come home feeling the singularity of an object; if it's handmade, all the better. White gives you the space to punctuate with personal objects, but some people find it cold and stark. Above all, let your home nurture you, let it hold you, let it be the one place you feel you can do very little wrong.

Join us at writing salon on Tuesday nights at the dollhouse,
suzannekingsbury.net

living in creative harmony

Rachael Rice: Artist, Musician, Creative Business Coach, Etsy Shop Owner
Lives in: Portland, Oregon
Describes her Style as: John Lennon. Cosmic. Bohemian.

"I don't get stuck in the idea of 'life balance'—for me, harmony is more important than "balance" which implies equity."

—Rachael Rice

Artist, teacher, musician, and creative business coach Rachael Rice has style and spunk. She packed up her bags and moved from Vermont to Portland, Oregon in pursuit of her creative career as a solo-preneur where she makes magical dream catchers and so much more. Her life, home, and art intermingle in one 650-square-foot space, a place of refuge, creativity, and above all, freedom.

Tell me a bit about you . . .
I live in Portland, Oregon and am a full-time creative, specializing in art instruction, music production, and creative business coaching with a very active Etsy shop.

How does your work stimulate creative expression in your home?
My home is also my studio and my office, so I strike a balance between super organized with all my supplies and having some of them strategically on "display" which also makes them handy.

As a multi-passionate creative how do you manage to juggle it all and thrive in your work/home?
I don't get stuck in the idea of "life balance." For me, harmony is more important than "balance," which implies equity. So I might spend a disproportionate amount of time in one creative area of my life for months at a time, but if it supports my overall vision, that's ok.

What inspires you?
Most of the furniture and stuff in my home is salvaged and repurposed. I try not to buy much that's "new"—there are already so many great used items in the world.

How does your home reflect your dreams, aspirations, and desires?
I live in about 650 square feet with my boyfriend. We keep our home situation multi-purpose, small, and affordable. We rent. This gives us a tremendous amount of freedom.

Do you have a favorite place in your home that makes you feel like you are thriving in your Sweet Spot?
My living room/studio/office/bedroom.

Anything else you'd like readers to know?
White lacquer paint is your friend. Mirrors. If you *love* it, it will look good.

Check out "this one woman creative tsunami" online at rachaelrice.com and see what she's creating over at etsy.com/shop/cosmicamerican

dreaming of the day

Desha Peacock: Mother, Author, TV Host, Founder of Sweet Spot Style

Lives in: Brattleboro, Vermont

Describes her Style as: Eclectic. Inviting. Personal.

"When someone says my home is a reflection of me, I take that as a compliment. That's the goal."

—Desha Peacock

Lying in the tiny twin bed listening to Loretta sing "Fist City," I heard a loud popping noise. "What was that?" I asked. "A gunshot," he said. "But don't worry, it's *outside*." You know it's a bad sign when you are comforted by learning the gunshot came from *outside!*

Our neighborhood in Little Rock, Arkansas, was too nice to be called the ghetto, but still, we were close enough to hear gunshots.

We called the one room garage "the cabin," because that sounds a lot more romantic than garage apartment.

We were finishing up our degrees (Matt's second one), and the rent was just right at $100 a month. Even though the neighborhood was sketchy and the only separation from the bedroom and toilet was a thin curtain, it didn't matter. We were young and newly in love. I liked his sensibility and the way he decorated with rocks, feathers, and old cameras. I loved listening to his scratchy records and

watching him pedal off to the university in his purple vintage Murray Wildcat. And that twin bed? It just made us a little closer. Smile.

I had always dreamed of living in a big 1920s craftsman style home in the historic neighborhoods of Hillcrest or The Heights. As a child, my mother and I drove through those tree-lined streets and wondered what each home held inside. It was more than just brick and mortar, wood and stone—it was the dream of being the kind of person who could live in such a lovely home, in such a lovely neighborhood. I imagined artists, writers, professors, doctors, and other *happy* people living in these homes. After graduating, I got my first job at Head Start and I was determined to move away from our ghetto-cabin. It was okay with me that we had to live in the absolute worst house in Hillcrest. At least it was Hillcrest.

When I asked Ms. Tucker, the landlady, if we could rip up the carpet in the kitchen and bathroom *(who in their right mind puts carpet in the kitchen and bathroom anyway?)*, she gave me a drunken smile and said, "You renters are all the same. This is an oooolllldddd house. You think you can just add some paint, rip up some carpet. . . . This is an oooolllldddd house."

"Well, yes, Mrs. Tucker, I do think that might help. I'll buy the paint," I said.

We lasted about a year in that Hillcrest house. We did rip up the carpet, and we painted the walls. Our friend made us a wooden tatami table. We added real red roses. Things seemed ok until the day I peed on the rat.

The toilet bowl was so little and low and the rat *so* big that to this day I can't go to the bathroom without looking first.

After that, the house reeked of dead rats to the point where I could no longer stomach it and once again, we moved.

This time it was 4505 Lee Avenue. A two-bedroom house with hardwood floors, two bathrooms, a front porch, garden, a sunroom and yes, it was in Hillcrest.

I don't live in Hillcrest anymore. I don't live in Arkansas anymore. I still cherish those 1920s craftsman homes and it warms my heart to hear my daughter's footsteps scramble down the large wooden staircase in the home of my dreams—here in Vermont—complete with gardens and a fireplace and *without gunshots or rats.*

And now to answer my own questions . . .

How does your home reflect your lifestyle, values, and what's important to you?

As a highly empathetic, intuitive person, I'm very tuned in and affected by my surroundings, from the people I associate with, to the clothes I wear, to the home I live in. Thus I'm consciously striving to create a life that brings me the most meaning, joy, and energy. I surround myself with people that inspire me, who share their gifts and make me laugh. Likewise, it's vital to have my home be a beautiful place that welcomes me, that makes me feel most myself and brings comfort to me and my family.

When people tell me my home looks and feels like "me," I take this as a compliment. I strive to make my home warm, cozy, and a place to relax and feel taken care of. Creative expression is something I value. In my home, you will see lots of art. Some of it is mine—bits of pottery I made in college, Chinese brush paintings I made when I was pregnant with my daughter, stenciled graffiti on aged wood by hubby. And lots and *lots* of my daughter's art. I love children's art because there is no ego. It's pure expression and it delights me. You will also find lots of art made by my friends—a ceramic bird by Erin Larkin, collage paintings by Corri Bristow-Sundell, woolly quilts by Rebekah Teague. Each of these items comes with a story and reminds me of how important it is for me to be around other creative souls. It feeds me and inspires me.

Have you created the space you love on a budget you can afford?

Oh yes I have! I have always been a thrifty shopper. It started as a necessity and now it's just part of who I am. I love the thrill of finding a deal. I get a kick out of saving money. My entire home is filled with thrifted and free finds. If I'm going to splurge, it's probably going to be on a handmade piece of art by someone I want to support, or a rug I've picked up in Guatemala or Tunisia. I can't seem to resist rugs or pottery when I travel. I've even gone so far as to carry three huge rugs rolled up in a garbage bag across my back on the New York subway after travelling across Central America. Heaven help me.

What's one thing that makes your heart sing?

I love that my home is filled with my daughter's friends. I love that they never want to leave because they are comfortable and have fun here. I love that I am able to give my daughter what I craved as a child—a beautiful, almost magical place with endless art supplies, hiding places, and history. I love to sit by the fire, drink tea or red wine, and watch the snowfall from my window in the cold Vermont winter. I love to sit on my front porch and marvel at the way plants and flowers seem to burst forth here in the spring after all that cold. I love when old friends come for dinner and we reunite over candlelight.

How does your home reflect *you*, your dreams, aspirations, and desires?

My home is a direct reflection of these things. Read the "Manifest Your Dream Home" chapter and you'll understand why.

chapter 3

USING COLOR TO CREATE THE FEELING YOU DESIRE

Have you ever tried on a mood ring? Supposedly, the color of the ring changes with your mood. Black means you are depressed, blue is calm, green is jealous, etc.

Whether you believe in mood rings or not, it's true that color can affect how you feel in a room. However, not everyone responds to color in the same way. For one person, red might evoke a sensual feeling, while for others it may be too intense and evoke a feeling of panic. White might be calming for some, while cold and institutional to others. Personality type and career may also play a role in how one is affected by color. For example, a fashion designer or artist who works in color and pattern all day long might be drawn to a neutral home environment or office which could offer less distraction and a sense of peace after a long day saturated in color. Yet for a nurse or doctor who works in a somewhat sterile environment, they may need to come home to bright or warm colors to either energize or soothe.

One of the strongest factors that influences a reaction to color is culture. For example, in Western societies white implies purity and innocence and is widely used in weddings. Whereas in China and India, white is representative of the state of mourning.

While my personal belief is that you should choose color based on what you are naturally drawn to and like, there are many studies that suggest color can impact our feelings and lives significantly. According to the principles of Feng Shui, color can play a role in helping to obtain love, prosperity, tranquility, joy, good health, and more. On the flip side, it can also over-stimulate, depress, and cause bad fortune.

In these pages, I've included a few common color meanings from both a Western and Eastern approach. Use this information as a general guide, knowing that your reaction to color might not be the same as listed here and you should always use your gut instinct as your primary guide.

FARMERS ALMANAC/COLOR THEORY (WESTERN)

RED

Intense. Love. Caution. Passion. Beware. Red is a very emotional color. It is supposed to stimulate a faster heart beat. Red is love. Red is a good color to use for accents in the home. Use caution when using in a child's room as it can over-stimulate.

YELLOW

The color of the sun, yellow invokes optimism, youth, fun, and good cheer. While it's usually associated with upbeat, optimistic, and sunny feelings in the west, studies reveal that when a room is painted bright yellow, it may cause a rise in bad temper and can increase irritability and crying in babies. Therefore, you want to avoid strong bright yellows in the nursery and bedroom. Use a lighter version such as cream in those areas.

BLUE

Blue is associated with tranquility, loyalty, wisdom, and trust. A popular color for bedrooms, blue invokes the sea and sky and is known to relax and help concentration. Use in the bedroom, nursery (lighter and pastel blues), sitting room, study, bathroom, or spa. If the color is too dark the impression created can be depressing and cold unless used with other warming colors and textures. Avoid in dining rooms or areas where there is a lot of activity, unless you would like to call in tranquility to those areas.

GREEN

Green is associated with nature, growth, money, fertility, and safety. Green is easy on the eye and can improve vision. It also has a calming effect and is often associated with good health and environmental sustainability. It is good to use anywhere in the home.

ORANGE

Vibrant orange calls for attention and stimulates, whereas a warmer orange feels more tropical and carefree. Terracotta is a very earthy, warm, and soothing color. As with any bright color, it can cause irritability if used widely.

PURPLE

The color of spirituality and royalty, purple is often well-liked by creative or eccentric types as well as adolescent girls.

PINK

A mix between sensual and vibrant red and innocent white, pink is often associated with romance and young girls in the west. Pink is the color of happiness, can be lighthearted, and for some overworked or overburdened women pink may speak of a desire for the more carefree days of childhood. Bright pinks are known to stimulate energy, while soft pinks can reduce erratic behavior.

GRAY

Gray is the color of dignity and carries authority. It is sleek and refined. Like white, it can seem cold and institutional and is good to use with other warm colors and textures. Because it's equal parts black and white, gray is the color of compromise. It's the perfect neutral, which makes it a great background color in home design.

WHITE

Used widely in weddings in the United States, white is associated with innocence, purity, freshness, and goodness. White is very trendy now, but may seem cold and institutional to some. Use a variety of whites to soften and add warmth to an all white room.

BLACK

Sometimes associated with evil (black holes, black capes), black is a powerful color that adds a sense of depth and style. It can also invoke authority, power, elegance, and style.

FENG SHUI (EASTERN)

Key to Feng Shui Elements	
Fire	Passion and High Energy
Earth	Nourishment and Stability
Metal	Clarity and Preciseness
Water	Ease and Abundance
Wood	Vitality and Growth

RED (FIRE)

In Feng Shui, vibrant red is a strong fire element and brings into your home the energy of joy and excitement. It also invigorates sexual desire, so would be a good addition in the master bedroom. Red is the Chinese color of luck and happiness, the marriage color in India, and the symbolic color of love and romance, courage, and passion in the West.

YELLOW (BRIGHT YELLOW IS FIRE, SOFT YELLOW IS EARTH)

According to the principles of Feng Shui, yellow offers a cheerful and uplifting feeling and can brighten any home or office. Yellow also creates cozy, welcoming Feng Shui energy in your kitchen, living room, or children's rooms.

BLUE (WATER)

From clear sky blue to soft aqua blue of the ocean and deep indigo blue, there is an endless variety of blue color tones that offer calm and tranquility. Great for bedrooms.

GREEN (WOOD)

Green represents renewal, fresh energy, and regeneration. Green is also associated with nourishment and health as it balances the whole body by bringing healing Feng Shui vibrations from nature.

ORANGE (BRIGHT ORANGE IS FIRE, SOFT ORANGE OR TERRACOTTA IS EARTH)

Less intense than red, orange is often called the "social" color, as it creates the necessary Feng Shui energy to promote lively conversations and a jolly nature in your home.

PURPLE (FIRE)

Vibrating on a high spiritual level, purple is often used in a healing or meditation room. Feng Shui masters advise using purple in moderation.

PINK (BRIGHT, HOT PINK IS FIRE, SOFT PINK IS EARTH)

Pink is the universal color of love, which makes it a perfect Feng Shui color to soften the energy in any given space. It offers a gentle, soothing, and delicate vibration suitable for any room in your home.

GRAY (METAL)

Often viewed as dull, in Feng Shui gray is considered sophisticated, upscale, and elegant if chosen wisely.

WHITE (METAL)

In Feng Shui, white is an expression of metal and this color represents purity and innocence. It is also considered a supreme color in ancient yogi traditions. Its energy is crisp, clean, and fresh and is suitable to brighten any room in your home. Having all white in your bathroom or meditation space can help soothe your psyche and spread healing vibrations through your home.

BLACK (WATER)

Representing the Feng Shui element of water, black offers mystery and sophistication. The color of midnight, deep dark waters, and the universal void, black adds depth, strength, and definition. In home décor, use it sparsely to add grounding and stability.

To learn more about the meaning behind colors, search online for Color Theory, Psychology of Color, Feng Shui/home décor and the Farmer's Almanac. Sensationalcolor.com is a particularly useful site.

Note on Color Variation

It is important to remember that the value (varied lightness and darkness) of a color can dramatically change a color's effect on a room's ambience. For example, red can denote passion, but if it's a really dark red it may denote fear (resemblance to blood or sirens), or if the red is lightened to a pink, it may denote charm and girlishness.

Choosing a Color Pallette for Your Home

When I first moved into my home I was overwhelmed by all the rooms I needed/wanted to paint. There was the kitchen, dining room, living room, office, two bathrooms, and three bedrooms upstairs. The upstairs could wait, but most of the rooms downstairs had really bad—I mean *really* bad—wallpaper that had to go, and the sooner the better. It was overwhelming and I wasn't sure where to start. A marketing friend of mine gave me some great advice that I'd like to share with you.

Knowing that I like art, my friend asked me what my favorite piece was in my home. I showed her a group of paintings that I bought from Etsy that I was in love with. They contained pale neutrals of washed out vintage colors. She held them up and said, "This is your pallette." Every single color I painted downstairs came from the pallette of those paintings which still hang in my dining room. Easy-peasy.

To learn more about how color can help you create your Sweet Spot, I've invited Artist and Color Expert Louise Gale to help you dive deeper into color sensing.

Color Exploration

Take a look at these colors and write down how each of them feels to you. What does each remind you of? Can you think of words you associate with these colors and what kind of feelings or emotions come up?

Now perhaps try it the other way around. Take a look at the list of words below. What colors do your associate with this list? What memories, events, or places do you associate with them? Be as descriptive as you can. Remember, this is personal to you.

Tranquil	Loving	Annoyed
Calm	Relaxed	Balanced
Happy	Passionate	Free
Smart	Friendly	Abundant
Creative	Angry	

Example: Tranquil might be "ocean blue, spa visits, beach, quiet, breeze, waves . . ."

Now take a look at your list. How can you incorporate more of the colors that make you feel good and less of the colors that make you feel bad?

In the following activity, I invite you to open up and let your intuition guide you; let it help you connect with the right colors to evoke the feelings you crave. Here's an example to help you get started:

FEELING YOUR ENVIRONMENT

Let's start by reading this statement out loud:

"I intuitively know what colors are good for me and I invite them into my home to create the haven I desire. My Sweet Spot Style colors will show themselves to me."

Now draw the table on the facing page onto a piece of paper or in your sketchbook/journal and add all the rooms and main areas of your home in the first column. Then take a little tour of your home. In each room, close your eyes and envision your room and how you want to feel in it.

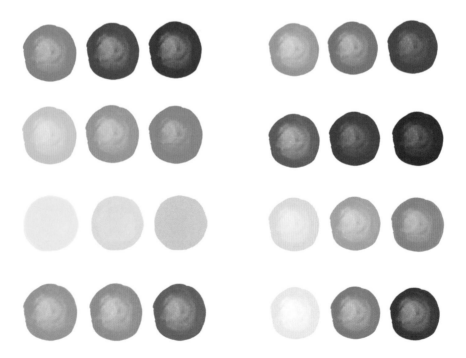

Room	Purpose	How I would like this space to feel?	Colors to introduce	Colors to take out	Notes:
Bathroom	*Cleanse, renew*	*Tranquil, clean, calm, close to nature, like I am in a spa!*	*Ocean blue, aquamarine green, white, natural elements.*	*The black shelving. (maybe repaint)*	*Add natural objects– sponge, painted stones, maybe some shells from the beach house.*

Ask yourself these questions:

❖ What will I be using this room for? Is it to relax, to work, to play?

❖ How do I want to feel in this room? How do I want my family to feel and others who visit?

❖ Does this room currently give off that feeling/energy? If not, what does my intuition tell me about this room? Is there a particular color I already have in this room that is creating a strange vibe?

❖ What colors would I like to see in this room? How much of this color or colors can I envisage?

Style note: This is just to get you started with feeling and connecting with color, so don't think too much about the colors you are writing down and their meanings. This is your personal space so there is no right or wrong. To add real energy to this exercise you could collect some paint chips, found objects from nature, or perhaps your favorite dress or artwork and carry these items around with you, really getting the feel for each color and any tones or shades you are particularly drawn to, imagining how they would make you feel in the room.

Creating Harmony in Your Spaces Using the Color Wheel

The color wheel is a useful tool for making sure the colors you choose will create harmony in your space.

COOL AND WARM COLORS

Yellows, oranges, and reds are warm colors. Greens, blues, and purples opposite them on the color wheel are cool colors. One way of creating harmony or balance is to use warm colors if you have a room that is in the cold or shady part of the house. For a room that is constantly in the sun, you might want to introduce cool colors.

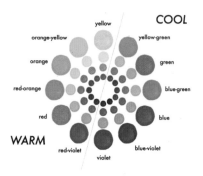

MONOCHROMATIC COLORS

This harmony uses four different values of the same color, from light to dark.
Pallettes that incorporate several shades of the same basic color are generally restful and calm while still offering enough variation to make a room interesting.

Light colors are airy, expansive, and cheerful. They can be used in small, dark areas to help them appear larger and brighter. Dark colors can create a cozy and sophisticated feeling in larger rooms.

• • • •

Add elements of nature to feel grounded and balanced. You can look outside your front door, or go for a walk in the woods or by the sea for inspiration.

Creative activities:

❖ Pop down to your local hardware store or paint shop and collect paint chips/samples in your colors.

❖ Create a series of "color love" pages in your journal or as a mood board to get to know your colors and to fall in love with them. You can use magazine cutouts, paints, and photographs.

❖ Arrange your color swatches in various ways to see which combinations feel great to you.

Consider making a color love journal for full visual saturation and color exploration, like this one by by artist and color expert Louise Gale.

Creative Tip:

Revisit or create a new mood board for each room (as we did in chapter 4). Use images, colors, and words to create a vision of how you want to feel in each room.

BOTTOM LINE: Color theory is fascinating, but at the end of the day the best way to choose color is by using your own inner guide, or intuition. To get you started, start pinning images on Pinterest as we discuss in chapter 4 ("Have a Vision!". Over time you will start to see a pattern emerge which will give you confidence when choosing the perfect color scheme for your home.

We typically think of a mood board as a piece of paper with images glued on, but they can be so much more, as you see from Erin Lorenzen's mood board shown here!

HAVE A VISION! CREATING MOOD BOARDS BY HAND OR ONLINE

What Is a MOOD BOARD?

A Mood Board is a collection of images and textures that creates a visual representation of a feeling or *mood*. Mood boards can be used for anything from finding your ideal career path to visualizing the love of your life to manifesting your innermost desires. In this book, we are focusing on mood boards to inspire you to live in your Sweet Spot in a very special place, your *home*.

Have you ever tried to describe a color? I remember trying to find a bath mat for my mother for Christmas. She said she wanted "green." So, I call her from my cell phone in Target. "Did you want sort of an olive green, mint green, hunter green . . . sea foam green??" She responds, "Something in-between." I picked the one I liked and hoped for the best. But the truth is that color evokes an array of feelings based on each individual's perceptions, emotions and memories associated with a particular color, or set of colors.

What do you think of when you hear the words "forest green"? For me it conjures Ralph Lauren's "Polo" brand in the 1980s—I see it paired with some stately Mahogany furniture and dark plaids. Maybe there are a few wooden ducks on the mantel.

Other terms for Mood Board include: Inspiration Board, Color Board, Story Board, or Design Board

It can be hard to imagine what a room or space will look like, so use mood boards to collect items that inspire you for a particular room and see how the items work together.

How about a pastel sea-foam green? What do you see? I see a beautiful pair of $300 pants with a black and white striped shirt I saw at Anthropologie—gorgeous combo! But I also think of someone's grandma's bathroom in Florida with bad shell wallpaper and shag carpets for bath mats.

The point is that trying to describe something that is visual and textural is very personal and can be difficult. Making a mood board not only clarifies your direction, it also takes your feelings, senses, and mood into account, helping to solidify one cohesive visual guide.

This mood board was created by Ashley Pahl, founder of the lifestyle blog *She Makes a Home* and *Snowed In* Magazine. "I made this moodboard to help inspire how I'd like to feel while I'm working from home. I want my surroundings to feel productive, inspiring, organized, and beautiful. It represents a space that I can both work in and relax in.

Three Ways to Make a Mood Board

LET YOUR VISION GUIDE YOU

You might know exactly what you want and then search for images and textures to match your inner vision. Be open to finding unexpected pieces that follow this vision through color, texture, or balance.

LET YOUR EYES GUIDE YOU

You might decide to simply start searching and see what you are naturally drawn to visually. Let the images guide you.

LET YOUR FEELINGS GUIDE YOU

Ask yourself "How do I want to *feel* in this space?" Perhaps you can write down the words and let them guide you. What would calm look like? What would energized look like? What would creative feel like?

PLAY! GET CREATIVE! TAKE YOUR TIME! GET INSPIRED! HAVE FUN!

Creating Virtual Mood Boards

With the plethora of images available on the internet, your choices are endless when it comes to creating a virtual mood board. Not only can you access millions of images, you can also quickly make and share your mood board online, which might be helpful if you want to incorporate certain paint colors, furniture, or accessories.

While you can use Microsoft Word to make a mood board, it's a bit cumbersome and time consuming. Photoshop works too, if you have it.

Use a mood board to help you edit. Think of yourself as a curator rather than a collector.

Technology is rapidly changing, but here are my favorite tools to make virtual mood boards.

MY FOUR FAVORITE, FREE, VIRTUAL MOOD BOARD TOOLS
Pinterest
With over 48 million users, Pinterest is here to stay. People love Pinterest because it is a visual bookmarking and virtual organization system. While awesome for home décor, it can also be used help you catalog any genre from your favorite recipe resources to your tech wish list and everything in between.

If you haven't tried it yet, it works like this: you make "boards" and label them into categories such as FASHION, or MY LIVING ROOM PAINT COLORS, or DREAM KITCHEN, and then you "pin" images from the web onto your board under the proper category. Once you pin an image to your board you can go back at any time and click on the image, which takes you back to the place you found it.

This system is genius for finding things quickly. Have you ever started browsing online looking for one thing, say a particular bed, but then *oopa*—you happen to see your dream couch but you know it's too expensive so you keep looking for the bed? But then a few days go by and you keep thinking about that darn couch and it takes you an hour to find it again online? Or, you're smart and you bookmarked it, but you have to scroll through the hundreds of other bookmarks you have also labeled "dream couch." Frustrating, right?

This is where the miracle of Pinterest comes in. You go to *one* place— Pinterest—and you find your *one* board on DREAM COUCHES and there you see all the "pinned" couches you've ever seen and loved online. You click on the picture and it takes you to the website you originally found it on. Love it! It's also a great way to compare products and prices. So you found that dream

Mood boards are all about capturing a thought, impression, theme or feeling.

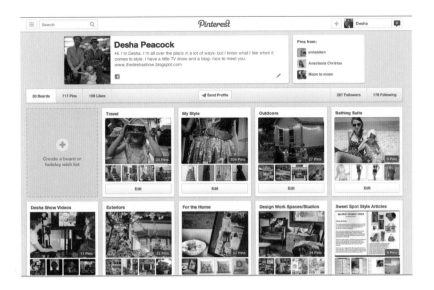

couch and it's $5,000 but then you search ebay and Etsy and you find a similar couch for $1,000. Boom! You can compare them side by side on Pinterest. Easy Peasy Lemon Squeezy.

Signing up for Pinterest is free and easy. You're ready to join, aren't you?

Feeling a bit shy? Don't want someone to steal your million-dollar idea? You can also make secret boards for your eyes only. Or, you can invite your special peeps to take a look. For example, as I searched for inspiration for my new Sweet Spot Style website, I pinned other websites that got my attention and wrote little captions like "nice color scheme" or "cool header" and shared my private board with my website designer. I don't need or want the whole world to see how I'm creating my site—that's top secret, sista—but imagine how much easier it is to share visual design information via Pinterest rather than sending my designer a million links with descriptions. I'm no tech genius, but that's old school, baby.

Olioboard

Olioboard is free with registration and is a cool online app for creating mood boards for interior design/home décor. It's preloaded with more than ten thousand items and three hundred brands including Ikea, CB2, Crate and Barrel, West Elm, and many more. You can search for items via color, category, price, or upload your own items.

My Deco

Similar to Olioboard, My Deco is a mood board tool, which is already packed full of home decorating ideas and furniture. You can start using My Deco straight away, but if you don't register you're limited to the items in the site's library, so it's worth spending two minutes signing up. That way you can add endless items found on the web or add your own private photos.

Polyvore

Traditionally used for fashion mood boards, there is a growing home décor section with thousands of pieces already uploaded on the site. You can also upload your own images.

CREATING MOOD BOARDS BY HAND

Creating mood boards online is fun and easy, but there is something about making them by hand that feels so good! While there is an endless supply of images to put on your virtual board, you really are limited to *images*. When making a mood board by hand, you can add textures such as feathers, fabrics, stickers, or even a beautiful faded love note. I really enjoy making handmade boards because it is more tactile and sometimes you just need a break from the computer. Can I get an *Amen*?

Mood boards are very personal, they are meant to inspire you and give you direction. In a world where you can access anything at anytime, having this direction will guide you to your ultimate goal of creating a personal space that feeds you.

You can also use mood boards to discover your own personal style. If you make enough of them, you will start to see a pattern or theme emerge. You will naturally start to see what you are drawn to. Are you picking out images and

Other free photo editing systems that you can use to make collages and add text are: Picassa, Lightroom, Picmonkey, Pixlr, and Canva.

Here are a couple of examples of my own handmade mood boards that I keep in my favorite journal.

textures with neutral tones and nature-based textures? This is information! Are you drawn to bright colors and shiny textures? This is information!

If you have a small enough mood board or book you can take it with you when you are shopping. This is especially helpful if you are looking to decorate one room in your home and you are on a tight budget.

23 THINGS TO ADD TO YOUR HOMEMADE MOOD BOARD

1. Pretty paper
2. Your personal photos of friends, family, nature . . .
3. Stickers
4. Feathers
5. Notes
6. Paper clips
7. Fabric of all shapes, sizes, and textures
8. Buttons
9. Japanese Washi Tape, or any tape for that matter!
10. Ribbons
11. Children's art
12. Images from magazines or books
13. Online images you print
14. Dried leaves and flowers
15. Glitter
16. Paint
17. Small paintings
18. Stamps
19. Paint chips
20. Postcards
21. Watercolor
22. Jewelry
23. Any found objects!

Here is the original electronic mood board I made on Picmonkey and then pinned onto Pinterest to guide my inspiration while decorating my daughter Iyla's room. After collecting my images on Pinterest, I made a simple sketch (handmade mood board) to help me visualize placement in her room.

6 FUN WAYS TO MAKE A HANDMADE MOOD BOARD

We typically think of a mood board as a piece of paper with images glued on, but they can be so much more!

1. Traditional Mood Board: images on a piece of thick paper
2. Mood Board Book: a collection of images bound in a journal
3. Wall Mood Board: use a cork board covered in a gorgeous fabric or paper, and tack images and textures that can easily rotate
4. Swinging Mood Boards: hang images and textures on a thin wire across your wall, above your bed, or doorway
5. Giant Sketchpads as Mood Boards: I have several of these. These are great for when I need to get out lots of ideas, or for big projects.
6. MDF/Wooden Mood Boards: Make giant mood boards on MDF (Medium Density Fiberboard) or use sanded wood of any size and shape to construct a portable mood board.

Finally, the room is finished. Can you see how I incorporated pieces from my original mood board? The mango carved bookshelf comes from a local store and we found the vintage quilt for $6 at the Hospice. We are still searching for the rug and mirrored chest, but overall we are both quite pleased.

Say that you decide to go to a few thrift stores or tag sales. There might be many things to entice you—say a pretty little vase for twenty-five tiny little cents, or a big ikat rug at a great price . . . but the only problem is that you already have a wall full of pretty little vases and you absolutely don't need a giant rug, no matter how pretty and cheap it is. So, you refer to your mood board. Are these items part of your vision? Do they fit with your color scheme? If not, be brave and put down the vase and rug. Your goal is not to collect clutter, but to enhance your home in a meaningful way that delights your senses.

"Mood boards are very personal, they are meant to inspire you and give you direction. In a world where you can access anything at anytime, having this direction will guide you to your ultimate goal of creating a personal space that feeds you."

chapter 5

CREATING INSPIRED OUTDOOR SPACES

I love being outside, especially when the weather is nice and sunny. There are so many ways to make an outdoor space inviting. Just as it's fun to mimic the outdoors inside, it's equally enticing to pull indoor elements outside. For example, why not add a soft rug on your front porch? Add pillows to the wooden porch swing? Create a *cabin*, like I describe in chapter 10 for quiet moments with your girlfriends.

What are you using the space for? Would you like a place to take your afternoon tea in quiet solitude? Do you like to entertain and imagine a table full of friends under night lights and a tree canopy? Do you need a place to soak up the sunrays or prefer the shade?

Some of my very favorite Sweet Spots are the places just outside my home, which include my front and back porches, the garden, hammock area, and my cabin. In the following section I'll give you tips on how to create your own Sweet Spot outdoor space.

Porch

An icon of the South, the front porch is a treasured place of both solitude and socializing. For centuries folks have gathered on the front porch to have tea, drink a glass of wine or beer, sit in a rocking chair, or swing and relax. I grew up in the South and that southern heritage comes through in a few places in my life. Even after living in New England for ten years, I still maintain a bit of a Southern accent, still drink tea every day, and still love a front porch.

One thing that drew me to my home in Brattleboro, Vermont, is how there are identical porches on the front and back end of my home—double sweet! On the front porch we have a simple wooden swing, a children's table, and a glass top round table and set of six yellow wrought iron chairs. This is where we eat every meal in the summer. I also have a little chair and table for one in a nook on my front porch that is just for me—that's where I take my daily tea between

Having an outdoor table is perfect for small dinner parties on the front porch.

Add color to your porch with potted and hanging plants. Introduce a flowering vine such as this one to provide shade and privacy.

three and four. It's hot tea and a sweet treat, to be exact. This is my daily ritual that I enjoy mostly alone or sometimes with a girlfriend or with my little girl, who also has developed a taste for black tea and milk.

When I'm sitting outside on my porch, looking over my garden and having my tea and sweet treat, I'm truly in my Sweet Spot. I feel so grateful for time to stop, reflect, and savor the life I've created. It makes me feel lucky and thankful.

PORCH FURNITURE
Common front porch furniture can include a front porch swing, rocker, wrought iron or wicker chairs, or any sort of outdoor seating that is comfy and can withstand a bit of weather.

PORCH FLOOR

I use a cotton rug on my front porch that works fine, but you can also use a regular outdoor rug or stencil a pattern on your wooden floor for a rug-like look.

Garden

Think of the garden around your home like you would an accessory to your outfit. The garden adorns your home just as a beautiful necklace, ring, or bracelet would complement your outfit.

I've always dreamed of owning a home with lots of outdoor space including a thriving and lush garden. I found an intention statement dated May 13, 2007 that described the kind of home I wanted, "... to be surrounded with beauty and a lovely garden full of flowers." Only six months later we moved into our first home in October 2007.

Robin MacArthur's front porch calls for conversation and play.

Patio

The patio is also a great place to create a magical Sweet Spot. A patio can be made out of many different kinds of materials from stained concrete, brick, stone, pavers, flagstone, fieldstone, pea gravel, slate, or even mulch. The material you choose will depend on the intended use of the patio. For example, if you want to hang a hammock or add a heavy, stationary chair or table you could go for mulch or pea gravel but these materials would not be well suited for a dining table where the movement of chairs back and forth would disturb the integrity of the floor. Instead, you would want a solid surface such as slate or brick.

6 TIPS FOR CREATING AN INSPIRED OUTDOOR SPACE

1. Frame and hang pictures in protected areas such as under a porch.
2. Add weatherproof curtains on one side of your porch to add privacy and warmth.
3. Add paper lanterns to create a playful environment.
4. Add texture and warmth by using outdoor rugs and pillows.
5. Rock it, honey. Add a porch swing, rocker, glider, or hammock.
6. Create a magical effect with sparkling stringed lights, a simple idea that creates a big impact.

"HALF OF THE FUN IN OWNING A HOME IS BEING ABLE TO GARDEN AND CREATE BEAUTIFUL OUTDOOR SPACES."

—SUZANNE KINGSBURY

Robin MacArthur enjoys her own dreamy hideaway in the hills of Marlboro, Vermont, where summers take on a special kind of magic after a long cold winter.

chapter 6

I love the nostalgia and romance of French doors, and have always wanted them as part of my life. I started a little collection of French doors on my Pinterest page and began imagining them in my home. Did I need French doors?

No.

But let me tell you how adding French doors to my office helped me through a tough time. It was after I submitted my proposal for this book and before I had an answer. I was midway through Marie Forleo's B-School e-course on building a life and business that you love and trying to figure out how I could start my own business doing work I love. So I was in the middle of lots of projects with big learning curves that would require being able to put in a massive amount of energy without knowing what the result would be. It's really hard to put your heart, soul, and sometimes money into big projects without having any sort of guarantee what the outcome will be. And when your whole life feels that way, it can seem like you aren't getting anywhere or achieving anything. I'm a very visual person and I love to see results of my labor. Thus, when I looked at my own Pinterest board titled "I'd Like to Add French Doors to My Life," I was struck by an incredible desire to take action.

When hubby balked at adding French doors to my office for no apparent reason (couldn't we use that money towards a new furnace? Kitchen remodel? New coffee table???), my answer was that I simply *needed* to have a vision and see it realized in a short period of time. It was so satisfying to think I could transform my office and make that one wish come true. Plus, do you ever feel like you just need more fun and less critical thinking in your life? Can't we adults just do something fun for no real good reason every once in a while? I was desperately seeking just a touch of whimsy. I could see myself throwing open the French doors to the patio and letting the breeze in, pretending I was on some quaint little balcony in a village in France. Now that I think of it, adding French doors is much better than the alternative—I could have decided to find whimsy in a hot affair with some lush Spanish lover. Or I could have spent every cent of our savings and then some on a vintage yellow convertible (I totally want one of those, too). So you see, French doors are totally reasonable.

When I began my search for vintage French doors, I found the perfect pair right away. Perfect, except for the $2,000 price tag. I called my carpenter friend over and told him my idea. Couldn't we just go buy an old door at the local salvage place down the road and cut the door in half? How much would that cost?

The next thing I know, my buddy is carrying a big white door with two glass panes into my garage. Unbelievable. He found one and bought it for only $60! He cut that door right down the middle. I got super doooooooper lucky and found a vintage doorknob (with a keyhole and key that works!!) for only $50. I've been told these are hard to find and I believe it.

My buddy ripped out the window in my office and installed the French doors in two days. The whole project, including the materials and labor cost less than $800, and most of that was labor. If you are handy and can rip out a window and install a door you could save a big chunk. Still, I think that's a good price for making a lifelong dream come true, don't you?

THINK ABOUT IT

Do you have a home project that you've always dreamed of but didn't do it because you didn't have time, money, or energy? How will tackling this project on a budget you can afford add value to your life right now?

chapter 7

RESOURCE GUIDE

Now that you've been inspired by the stories and images of how others have created their own Sweet Spot Style and you are well-trained in how to put together your visual guide to make your own Sweet Spot home, it's time to *shop*. Oh yes, I see you smiling right now!

But don't worry; this book is not about putting together a "budget" of thirty thousand bucks to furnish your living room. If you've got that, hooray for you, that's awesome, go crazy! But, if you're like the rest of us folks, you can't go hog wild and spend every single dime you've earned on one gorgeous mirrored chest. But, does that mean you can't have fun and live in your Sweet Spot? Heck no! You can and you *will*.

Do you believe in magic?

Time vs. Money: What's It Gonna Be, Partner?

If you've got the cold hard cash to do whatever you want, you can seriously just go and buy it. But, caution, please don't buy some box set at Pottery Barn that has zero personality and little meaning. Take your time and shop around. Mix pieces to make your style unique and more diverse.

If you are on a super tight budget, not to worry, you can create a lovely space for free, but it's going to take time and work.

Now, here's the low down and dirty truth: it's either going to take time, money, or work, and that's final. If you've got the money, you might not have the time. Fine, just take enough time with your purchases to make sure you're getting what you really want. No need to wait five months to find the perfect chair that you'll need to sand and paint at the good ol' Salvation Army.

If you've got no cash, but you do have time, you're in luck—you *can* scour all the thrift stores and sand and paint those chairs that looked so grimy! Put up your before and after shots on your blog and wow the world!

Don't have time, money, or the desire to work? I don't know what to tell you. You're out of luck, my friend. But, here's the thing, I've been in both camps—I've had very little money at some points in my life and I've had a decent little budget (but less time) for home décor on a few occasions and I can tell you on both accounts I have made it work because I care. And if you care, you'll make it work, too.

Where to Shop When Your Greatest Asset Is TIME

As we've discussed, you are going to have to spend either time or money to make your Sweet Spot home. If you have the time, but limited resources, here are some places to shop that you will *love*.

TAG SALES

Tag sales, otherwise known as yard sales or garage sales, are great for finding unique and very well-priced treasures. If you are a die hard tag-saler you will scout them out the night before in the paper or on Craigslist, you will make a map of which ones to hit, you will pick the best neighborhoods, and you will wake up *very early* and be the first one there. Like any good sale, the really good stuff does go early. But, as much as I love me some tag sales, I love cuddling in bed and my morning tea and toast even more. Here's my approach: I get up when I want and I do a slow drive by in the "good neighborhoods." If I see potential, I hop out, take stock quickly, and then off I go to the next one.

I live in a small town in Southern Vermont where people have tag sales every single weekend in the summer. It's too dang cold and snowy to even consider having a tag sale any other time, so summer is the season for it here. If you live in a warm climate, you probably can find tag sales year-round. For those of you who live in very rural spots, tag sales might not be the best option for you unless you want to go every once in a while and make a day trip out of it just for fun. Again, you can't really have an agenda here. You go, you see, you

Believe it or not, I scored this wooden dining table for $10 at a tag sale in Brattleboro—it's perfect for art projects, dinner parties, or oatmeal! The refinished dining room chairs are from Sticks and Bricks in Northampton, Massachusetts, one of my favorite local boutiques.

assess. You might spend a couple of hours and find nada. You might go and find the perfect nightstand that needs a little paint for $5.

The best tag sale I ever went to was one that was in my neighborhood. I rarely am organized enough to check Craigslist for tag sales, but for some reason I did once. The description was something like, "Graduate student moving to Bali, lots of vintage furniture, lamps, and art." Now that was one that sounded worth getting up early for. I was the first person there. It started at 9am, which is unheard of! They usually start much earlier. Seemed like a sign that this chick would have good stuff. And sure enough, she did. Jackpot! I figured if she was moving to Bali she might be into international travel, which means she might already have some cool ethnic goodies.

Nearly everything in this room came from one awesome tag sale!

TAG SALE SHOPPING TIPS:

1. Go early.
2. Make a mental list of things you really need or want and try to stay focused. Only get something you can use now or that you absolutely love. Remember, we don't want to add unnecessary clutter to our homes.
3. If you see something you love but you don't need it, maybe you can still get it for a friend—just make sure you give it to someone who won't be put off by the fact that it's gently used.
4. Bring cash. Small bills and change are good.
5. Before purchasing something that needs lots of work, ask yourself if you will really do the work. Sanding, painting, recovering furniture—all of these things you can do but it will require time and effort.
6. It's ok to haggle. Prices are probably already low, but it's ok to ask for a better price, especially if you are buying several items. But remember, you are probably already getting a sweet deal, so over-zealous haggling is annoying.

MY FAVORITE TAG SALE SCORES:
Lovely linen covered chair with feather cushion: $40
A little soiled, but such a quality and comfy chair it would be silly to pass this up. I like the pattern, but I could get it recovered for around $250 later, if I want to.

Turkish wool rug: $20
Such a freakin' steal. Are you kidding me, these are *expensive*. The threads are a bit bare in places, but I think this adds to the charm, and I actually prefer them faded and worn.

Two pair of vintage Asian curtains: $40
These were a tiny bit pricey for curtains that are not in the greatest shape, but the pattern and weight of them sold me. One day I might take them down and make large cushions.

Metal black vintage lamp table set: $15
Score! I love this little reading lamp and I really needed one.

CRAIGSLIST

With over 50 billion page views per month, you probably already know that Craigslist is a great place to find used furniture, appliances, and other household items. Just like shopping at a tag sale or thrift store, you need to be patient using Craigslist, but the advantage here is that you can search from the comfort of your home, or mobile device.

Are you a risk-taker?

Although a bit more risky, we have bought appliances on Craigslist. I wouldn't recommend purchasing high priced items this way because chances are there's no warranty, so if something goes wrong and your $800 fridge conks out, you are up a creek. To help minimize risks, do some research by reading the reviews on the product beforehand. If an appliance is no longer being manufactured, use this to your advantage in the haggling phase. You should get a price break for things that aren't on the market as this means it might be harder to service. If it's clean, has good reviews, and it's cheap, it's probably worth it. For example, when we were looking for a new stove we couldn't find much under $500, but we did find a Hot Point stove for $50. You really can't go wrong with that price. Of course, it accidentally caught fire one year later and now we are searching for another one . . . so kind of glad we only spent $50 on that one!

Support local artists and economy by shopping local. Sticks N' Bricks is one of my favorite places to shop in Northampton, Massachusetts. Full of electric handmade items from local artists using repurposed materials and reclaimed wood, it's a great place to find a one of kind item.

"I paid $400 for this headboard, and later found out a friend of mine had talked them down to $300, but then her husband said no. I should've bargained!"says Sarah Sandidge of her Craigslist treasure.

TIPS FOR SHOPPING CRAIGSLIST

1. Look often.
2. Look outside of your area. For example, we live in Southern Vermont, but I'll often search in Western Mass and New Hampshire as there are bigger towns within a forty-five minute radius.
3. For home décor, it's faster if you click on the icon to see postings that only contain images—saves you a lot of clicking!
4. Search your smart phone for apps such as cPro that make browsing faster and more efficient.
5. Haggling is okay (within reason). For example, if you find a wooden dresser for $75 but it's a little banged up, ask the owner if they would be willing to take $60. You'll have better haggling results if you can pay cash and pick up the item quickly.
6. Bring a friend. Better safe than sorry.

THRIFT STORES

I love thrift stores! Why? For the same reason I love tag sales: when you find something you love for super cheap, it feels amazing! It's like you've won the game. You got lucky. You scored. Doesn't that feel good?

Here are some vital tips of the trade:

1. Go frequently.
2. Just like tag sales, have a list but be open if you find something you just really love.
3. Be ready to work. Sometimes there's a lot of sifting.
4. Visualize. You could find something awesome, but it might need a little paint.

THINGS FOR THE HOME THAT YOU CAN ALMOST ALWAYS FIND AT THRIFT STORES:

1. Silverware, cups, plates, dainty china
2. Vases of all kinds for incredibly cheap
3. Baskets
4. Curtains

I fell in love with this handmade pillowcase from Experienced Goods (my favorite thrift store in Brattleboro that supports our local Hospice system). I found the sweet vintage chair at a tag sale for $10 and the black metal side table was found free on the side of the road!

Common thrift stores include: The Salvation Army, The Goodwill, your local Hospice Store.

Like tag sales, it takes more time than money to find the right thing, so it's not for you if you are super busy or impatient.

ONE OF MY THRIFT STORE SCORES:
Handmade vintage cotton quilt

It's not terribly often that you find cotton handmade quilts at the thrift store. That's because scavengers buy these up quickly and sell them in the antique shop for hundreds of dollars. If you do get lucky and find one, they are probably either stained or made with funky material such as polyester. I'll pass on that. So, when I found a quilt for only $6, I grabbed it (see page 175 for photo). And bonus, I already knew I wanted a quilt like this for my daughter's room—it was even on my mood board. Double score! As I was walking through the store, two or three people commented on it. Hands off people, finders keepers!

VINTAGE/ANTIQUE STORES

What's the difference between shopping at a thrift store and a vintage/antique store? The price! They both have used items, but the difference is that you have to shuffle through a lot more stuff at the thrift store to find a gem. In a vintage/antique store, the owner has already done the shuffling for you and picked out the crème de la crème, so you don't have to get your hands dirty, if you know what I mean. Remember our little talk about time and money? Here, you are saving time, but you're going to have to pay for it, doll.

And I should make the distinction here, although the lines between vintage and antique are blurry, the term "antique" is generally used for items that are more than one hundred years old and "vintage" for items that are at least twenty-five years old and represent an era in which it was made. The word

"antique" implies that there is more value, simply because there is more demand for it. Rare antiques can be quite expensive. I tend to stay away from expensive antique stores, but I have found a few stores labeled "antique" that had decent prices. However, if I can find an item in a thrift store for $5, I'm not going to pay $50 in an antique store for the same piece. This is a personal decision because I am a thrifty shopper. Just raised that way. And I enjoy the thrill of getting something I know is worth more than what I paid for it. I do not enjoy the feeling that I bought something that I could have found for less. However, this means I spend more *time* finding my gems.

It's eco-friendly to shop at tag sales, thrift stores, vintage/ antique shops, and find things for *free*. If it's in your living room, it's not in the landfill, now is it? Congrats, yet another reason to feel proud of yourself. Nice job!

Consider using a variety of vintage plates to add charm and whimsy. Wouldn't these plates from Twice Upon a Time in Brattleboro look cute for your next tea party?

Overall, the difference between vintage and antique appears to be one of age and marketability. Antique furniture and other collectibles over one hundred years old are generally handled by professional antiques dealers, while vintage items are often bought and sold by private collectors or amateur enthusiasts.

Photographer Elle James collects vintage suitcases for storage or to pack for an overnight sleepover.

MY VINTAGE/ANTIQUE SCORES:
Sofa with Roller Legs: $500
Four Poster Bed: $125
Enamel Kitchen Table and Chairs: $200

FLEA MARKET
What exactly is a flea market and why on earth is it called that?
A flea market is basically just a market, typically outdoors, that sells
secondhand goods at reasonable prices. The concept has existed for thousands
of years, particularly in Asian countries like India, Bangladesh, and China.

Apparently the origin of the term "flea market" is disputed, here are a couple
of theories according to Wikipedia:

The traditional and most publicized story is in the article "What Is a Flea
Market?" by Albert LaFarge in the 1998 winter edition of *Today's Flea Market*
magazine. In his article LaFarge says, "There is a general agreement that the
term 'Flea Market' is a literal translation of the French *marché aux puces*, an
outdoor bazaar in Paris, France, named after those pesky little parasites of the
order *Siphonaptera* (or 'wingless bloodsucker') that infested the upholstery of
old furniture brought out for sale."

The second story appeared in the book *Flea Markets*, published in Europe by
Chartwell Books. The introduction states:

> In the time of the Emperor Napoleon III, the imperial architect
> Haussmann made plans for the broad, straight boulevards with rows
> of square houses in the center of Paris, along which army divisions
> could march with much pompous noise. The plans forced many dealers
> in second-hand goods to flee their old dwellings; the alleys and slums
> were demolished. These dislodged merchants were, however, allowed to
> continue selling their wares undisturbed right in the north of Paris, just
> outside of the former fort, in front of the gate Porte de Clignancourt. The
> first stalls were erected in about 1860. The gathering together of all these
> exiles from the slums of Paris was soon given the name "*marché aux
> puces*", meaning "flea market".

Discarded during a high school renovation, Sarah Sandidge found this very cool private door at a flea market for $100. I love the idea of placing it on sliders at the end of the staircase—great for keeping babies off those tempting stairs! The large green letter E was also a flea market score at just $25.

ETSY

You might know Etsy for all the handmade goodness and amazing art, but did you know you can also buy all kinds of handmade and vintage furniture and household items? Oh yes, it's true! I love Etsy!

You can find everything from amazing French headboards to vintage sofas to charming English teacups and so much more. Some categories that come up under Home & Living on Etsy include: Bars, Beds & Headboards, Cabinets and Bookcases, Desks, Dressers, Media Consoles, Mirrors, Seating, Sinks, Storage, Tables, and more. You have the option of searching for either handmade or vintage items within each category above.

My Favorite Etsy Shops: Now seriously, this whole book could be a list of amazing Etsy shops—there are that many great ones—but here is a short list of some of my personal favorites. Do you have a favorite Etsy shop? Tell me at SweetSpotStyle.com.

Home Décor

- Kokuun: etsy.com/shop/kokuun
- LittleByrdVintage: etsy.com/shop/littlebyrdvintage
- Rubbish Rehab: etsy.com/shop/RubbishRehab
- 3BModLiving: etsy.com/shop/3BModLiving

- LampShadeDesigns: etsy.com/shop/LampShadeDesigns
- Villarreal Ceramics: etsy.com/shop/villarrealceramics

Textiles
- Enhabiten: etsy.com/shop/enhabiten
- Skinny La Minx: etsy.com/shop/skinnylaminx
- Martha And Ash: etsy.com/shop/MarthaAndAsh
- Leah Duncan: etsy.com/shop/leahduncan

Art
- Peggy Wolf: etsy.com/people/PeggyWolfDesign
- Matou en Peluche: etsy.com/shop/matouenpeluche
- Chasing the Crayon: etsy.com/shop/ChasingtheCrayon
- Catherine Nolins: etsy.com/shop/CatherineNolinArt
- Studio Enrouge: etsy.com/shop/enrouge
- Rachael Rice: etsy.com/shop/cosmicamerican
- Dear Pumpernickel: etsy.com/shop/dearpumpernickel
- Sara Ahearn: etsy.com/shop/sarahearn
- Kelzuki: etsy.com/shop/kelzuki

Personalize your home with unique art finds, like these cosmic dream catchers by Rachael Rice (etsy.com/shop/cosmicamerican).

How to Get It FREE
EVER LOOKED ON THE SIDE OF THE ROAD?

In New England people just put out their old stuff and with a FREE sign on it. I really can't recall this happening in Arkansas. Is this a national thing, or am I just spoiled here? I'm not sure, but it is quite a phenomenon. I've found lots of goodies this way. My New York City friend gets most of her furniture free on the sidewalk. She says if it's out there, even without a sign, it's cool to take it. However, taking cushy chairs or beds

This print purchased from Etsy on Matou en Peluche rests on my mantel in the living room.

is a big no-no. Think bed bugs. If you live in a place that has lots of tag or yard sales, remember this little hint: go for a stroll after two or three o'clock on a big tag sale day (usually that's a Saturday) and you will see that everything that didn't sell is now on the side of the road with a FREE sign.

FREE side of the road scores
Velvet Green Wooden Chair
Vintage Horse Painting
Rattan Chair
Children's Patio Chairs
Vintage Metal Tray
Vintage Metal Table

FREECYCLE
freecycle.org
As defined on their website, "The Freecycle Network is made up of 5,104 groups with 9,419,061 members around the world. It's a grassroots and entirely nonprofit movement of people who are giving (and getting) stuff for free in their own towns. It's all about reuse and keeping good stuff out of landfills. Membership is free." Simply find your community online and sign up. Susie

Belleci, featured in chapter 2, is a diehard Freecycle fan. She's furnished 95 percent of her house with free items, many that she's found on Freecylce.

My scores from Freecycle
Living Room Sofa

THE DUMP

Yes ma'am, I'm not too good to be found at the dump. The word *dump* does not channel beauty or what you might think of as your Sweet Spot, but I'm telling you that if you go frequently enough, you can find some amazing treasures at the dump (I actually kind of like saying the word "dump"—it sounds so *trashy!*).

I found this green velvet chair with a free sign on it after a tag sale.

Our local dump holds a swap every Saturday until noon where you can peruse items donated by folks that normally would have ended up in the trash. You can find loads of stuff for free such as non-upholstered furniture, lawn and garden equipment, and household items including dishes, lamps, frames, utensils. If you are remodeling your home you might find sinks, counters, shelves, doors, windows, bricks, and lumber. Small appliances like toasters, irons, blenders, and mixers can be found as well.

The dump is a great place to find free stuff and to get rid of your old stuff, too. If it's been sitting in the basement for more than one year, please take it to the dump and as you say your sweet goodbye you can imagine the lit up face of some nice, old lady, young broke college student, or *me* standing there ready to offer it a nice loving home. Don't steal our joy—if you don't love it to death, pass it on to someone who will!

How to find the dump in your area? You can search online using keywords like *Waste Management*, *Landfill*, *Recycling Center*, or *Swap Shop*.

If you don't have a dump near you, try to remember to look for one while on vacation, especially capital cities or ritzy places like Santa Barbara or Martha's

Susie Belleci found both of these wooden chairs and the coffee table at the dump (or "swap shop," as she likes to call it—everyone else calls it the dump).

Vineyard. Once in Nantucket I found some great souvenirs including my favorite straw purse, a vintage tee shirt, and a dress. My hawk-eyed friend snagged the gorgeous hand woven wool rug before I could get to it. It was probably from Turkey or Morocco, or somewhere I'm dreaming of going. This brings me to my final piece of advice for shopping at the dump, tag sales, or vintage/antique stores . . . Be careful who you bring along, especially if you have similar taste. You might lose a friendship (or your arm!) over the perfect armchair, or an exotic wool rug, for example. Kidding (sort of).

FYI, if you live in an urban area, you might have more access to dumpsters than a dump. If this is the case, you could consider "dumpster diving." Yep, you are literally taking things from the dumpster itself. This is only for the brave at heart. However, that same New York City friend I mentioned above told me her best date was dumpster diving in the snow in Oxford. So, there you have it.

MY DUMP SCORES
Wooden Chairs . . . oh so many varieties!
Metal/wood children's desk
Gorgeous tea sets
Wine glasses galore!

When to SPLURGE!
You are on a budget, but you still want the best

According to a recent report form the *Boston Globe*, "The emphasis is changing from 'Where can I save the most money?' to 'What's the perfect piece that totally reflects me?'" "It's a nice shift," Rogowski of the Boston Design Center says. "It could be the economy, or it could be that people are ready for change."

One of the perks of being thrifty most of the time is that once in a while, when you find the right piece that reflects your aesthetic, you're probably willing and able to pay a little more for it. That's why I've included this section on "When to SPLURGE!"

There are lots of amazing handmade boutiques online. Look up Coral & Tusk and Powederhorn Kitchen to get started!

As you can tell, I'm good at getting stuff pretty darn cheap or free. What started out as a necessity became a fun game, and I still love the thrill of a deal. But I also have much less time than I used to. I'm a multi-passionate entrepreneur with a child and busy life, so while I love the thrill of the hunt, I also enjoy finding things that are brand new, unique, and utterly gorgeous—as is— with no sanding, painting, or "creative imagining"! Plus, there are times when I see something and I know it's worth it because it's totally me, fits perfectly in my home, or is something I've been looking for and haven't found at any of my bargain spots.

Get thyself unto the nearest local boutique and support thy local economy! One of my favorite places to shop is Altiplano in downtown Brattleboro. It's where I go for unique gifts, paper products, fair trade bags, and earrings designed by owner Shari Zarin.

There are a few places I like to shop, and although it's more pricey than *free*, I know it's worth it.

WHAT I'VE SPLURGED ON:
Not that much really. My bed is a fake foam bed, but it's comfy. It's new. And when I say "splurged," I really mean I paid more than I would if I found it at a thrift store or on the side of the road.
Mango Wooden Book Shelf, Adivasi
Chandelier Lighting, Lighting.com
Rugs: Spain, Guatemala, and Tunisia
Art: Etsy, private sales
Yellow Cabinet: Ikea (hardly a splurge, but it's new)
Hardware: Anthropologie
Dishes and Cups: Anthropologie

A word on Anthropologie: I really like this store. It's one of my favorites and they have good sales in the home department. To save the old wallet but still have the Anthro experience, I tend to buy smaller items there, such as hardware for cabinets, tea cups, dishes, and that sort of thing. They have lovely, unique furniture, curtains, and bath items as well. And the dresses . . . oh, we are not talking about dresses are we? Guess I'll have to save that for the

My vintage couch (front and center) is from an antique store in Northampton, Massachusetts. At $500 I consider it a pretty sweet deal (though not compared to my other couch to the right, which I found free on freecycle). My treasured chandelier was on sale for $250 from lighting.com and the rug came from Tunisia—I don't remember the exact price, but the cost of that trip set me back a pretty penny.

When my favorite tea cup from Anthropologie took a tumble, my daughter, knowing how much I love my Anthro tea cups, doctored it up and presented it to me with a smile, "It's all fixed, Momma!" True love.

next book on personal style. Wink, wink.

I would be a naughty girl if I didn't tell you that I have, and occasionally still do, shop at "box stores." Not only that—I have been known to pull over at Dunkin Donuts for a double chocolate donut. While my health nut hubby thinks I'm gross for doing it, my philosophy is "everything in moderation," and that goes for chain store shopping as well. While I don't advocate buying everything in your home from one chain store, I think a little bit of "box store" is ok. No judgment sisters— sometimes you just need some basics and you can find these things easily and very reasonably priced. And while you're at it, grab a donut on the way.

When looking for reasonably priced home décor items try these stores . . .

- Ikea (look for bookshelves, curtains, arm chairs, sofas, kitchen items, and outdoor items)
- Urban Outfitters (great for rugs, curtains, pillows, and other textiles)
- World Market (find very reasonable curtains, kitchen basics, and outdoor furniture)
- Target (search for lamps, pots, kitchen basics, frames, smaller home accessories)

Finding Inspiration Online, Best of . . .

Pinterest: We've already talked about how awesome Pinterest is for designing mood boards and it's also a great place to find inspiration for all your home décor projects. Type in key words such as *kitchen inspiration, girl's bedroom, gray walls, ikat fabrics* and find thousands of images to inspire you. Pin the ones you love the most on your board, label them, and you have a visual record of your inspiration.

While I'm a big fan of home décor books and magazines there is also an endless amount of content on décor related blogs. Blogs come and go, but there a few really great ones that are here to stay. Below are a few of my favorites.

FAVORITE BLOGS

- Decor8: decor8blog.com
- Design Sponge: designsponge.com
- Young House Love: younghouselove.com
- A Beautiful Mess: abeautifulmess.com
- Apartment Therapy: apartmenttherapy.com
- Dreamy Whites: dreamywhites.blogspot.com
- Happy Interior Blog: happyinteriorblog.com
- Dwell: dwell.com
- The Selby: theselby.com/about/
- Desire to Inspire: desiretoinspire.net
- Justina Blakeney: justinablakeney.com
- Miss Mustard Seed: missmustardseed.com
- The Design Conundrum: designconundrum.com
- She Makes a Home: shemakesahome.com
- The Inspired Room: theinspiredroom.net
- Apartment 34: apartment34.com/category/decor/
- Byfryd: byfryd.com

DESHA'S 6 TIPS FOR CREATING YOUR OWN SWEET SPOT STYLE HOME

1. Finding the right thing for the right price takes time, but it's worth it. Be patient.

2. Don't be afraid of work. There are many things you can learn to do in your home that will save lots of money. You can paint, rip up carpet, sand the floors, reupholster wooden chairs, and take down wallpaper. I promise you can!

3. Purchase or make original art for your home to give it a personal touch.

4. Take it room by room. Having too many projects going on in the home can be overwhelming and add to a sense of chaos. Pick one room or one project at a time. *Finish* it. Then repeat.

5. Create at least one space in your home or outdoor area that makes you feel like you are in your Sweet Spot. Go there often and be grateful for it.

6. Understand that it's a process. If you want to creatively express yourself in your home, you must understand that you are a changing being, and thus your home décor will also need to adjust and change as you do. What I'm saying is that you are really never finished, so just go ahead and enjoy the process.

When people ask me if I'm an artist, I never know what to say. I've dabbled in pottery, painting, knitting, collage, and some of these experiments end up around my home, such as the two little Chinese brush paintings on the left. The vintage wall cabinet is from Sticks and Bricks in Northampton, Massachusetts. The small vases are a mix of found milk jars and handmade vessels from Tunisia. Flowers from the garden add color and life.

chapter 8

"Let your spending be a prayer for what you love and for what you desire—for yourself, for your family, and for the planet."

—Kate Northrup Moller, Author of *Money, A Love Story*

I value both time and money. I find ways to creatively express myself in my home by not going over budget and staying within my means, which means it often takes time, but not too much time because I have other things I love like my family, friends, travel, and fashion!

In Chapter Two, we learned through the case studies how important personal values are and how the way we decorate should be in alignment with those values. One of my personal values is to have enough money to feel free and to do the things I desire. But when making money starts to interFEAR with my lifeSTYLE—in other words, if *all* my TIME goes into making MONEY—then I'm not enjoying LIFE. So, it's a delicate balance isn't it?

Another value is that I choose not to live beyond my means. Oh sure I could take out a $15K loan and get the kitchen I want now. I could whip out the ole' credit card and buy all the newest spring fashions from Anthropologie. But then I would be in debt, and debt is not freedom. Debt = the opposite of freedom and it's just not worth it. So that's why I often go the extra mile to find things that I love that are beautiful, but that I'm able to afford. Staying within my financial means makes me feel like I'm living in my Sweet Spot.

More DIY Money Saving Tips

There are money saving tips sprinkled throughout this book, but in this section I'd like to share a few secrets that help me stay on budget when it comes to creating my Sweet Spot home. In addition to all the thrifty shopping I do, there are a couple of other ways I have found to ease the ole' wallet. Everything I'm sharing here are things that I've actually done in my home. I promise if I can do it, so can you.

TO SLIPCOVER OR NOT?
Is it Worth it?
Here's the deal—you can buy brand new furniture that looks good at places like Ikea and West Elm for so little that it might be cheaper to buy new furniture than to have it slipcovered or upholstered by a professional. There are many factors that go into the decision of whether to upholster or slipcover a piece, including if you do the work yourself or hire out, how much you will spend on the furniture you want to recover, the quality and "bones" of the piece you want to recover, the cost of the fabric, and how much time you have for the project.

> I'm not a big fan of the slouchy "throw a sheet over it" look, so I don't recommend buying ready made slipcovers unless you check the measurements of your piece for a proper tailored fit. Ill-fitting slipcovers are the worst!

Upholster or slipcover?
It depends on the look you want and how much use the piece will get. Upholstery is the most tailored look, although it's possible to get a very tailored look from a slipcover. I am going to focus on slipcovers because they are easier to change and keep clean.

Slipcover it yourself or leave it to the pro?
It's totally possible for you to learn how to slipcover furniture. I've done it on footstools and dining chairs, but when it comes to a sofa or living room chairs, I prefer a tailored look that I don't have the time *or patience* to learn. Therefore, I prefer to send those bigger, bulkier pieces to a professional. But don't let that stop you from trying it yourself!

Save money by starting with what you have, or free furniture finds

My eyes are always peeled for roadside furniture finds, so when I saw a cute little love seat with a free sign on my very own street I just had to stop. First, I checked out the bones, which were in good order. No broken legs, firm but comfy cushions, no bad odor such as smoke or animal scents (which can be hard to remove). The fabric was not my favorite and had some stains and rips, but the structure was good and I could live with the fabric for a spell.

You've heard of women who can lift a car to save a child who is underneath, right? Well, I've been known to get that adrenaline flow when it comes to free furniture. I popped the thing in the back of my Subaru and off we went!

REMINDER: CAREFUL WITH PICKING UP FREE STUFF!

When picking up free furniture, it's better if you already have a place to use it in mind—otherwise you might end up with too much and nowhere to put it. We want to avoid that! In this case, I knew I wanted a loveseat in my daughter's room because we needed a new reading space and I loved the idea of curling up with her nightly to read on a pretty little loveseat.

My daughter's slipcovered couch with drop cloth fabric was inspired by the *Miss Mustard Seed* Blog. Slipcover made by Lori Palmer of Coverings in Brattleboro, Vermont.

Watch your budget

I knew I wanted a slipcover for my loveseat because we have bedtime snacks while reading, but when I discovered the cost of the fabric per yard and the cost of a custom slipcover, I realized I could buy a brand new couch from Ikea for the same price. However, this free couch was probably more comfortable than an Ikea piece and I like the idea of keeping big bulky items out of the landfill when possible.

I got a quote for $330 from a local lady who has a good reputation for making slipcovers. The price included all the pillows and a little demi ruffle that I thought was sweet for my daughter's room.

Choosing your fabric

The next step was finding fabric. There are so many gorgeous fabrics out there that it can be truly inspiring, but also overwhelming. I found loads of gorgeous Chinoiserie fabrics that would make a stunning cover, but some of them were hundreds of dollars a yard! Of course there is a big range, but you would be hard pressed to find a quality fabric for under $7 a yard. I did manage to find a pretty cotton fabric online for $7.50 a yard. I needed fifteen yards, so that would have cost $112.50, plus shipping and handling.

But I was nervous the cotton would be too thin and not hold up. I wanted a heavy weight fabric for my project because this particular piece would get lots of wear and tear in my daughter's room (not as much as if I had a rambunctious couple of boys—my daughter is pretty dainty—but still she likes to jump and that kind of thing!)

I checked into buying a more sturdy canvas fabric (there are several varieties including brushed canvas which is a little softer and duck fabrics which are stiffer). Prices ranged from $5 a yard to $12 a yard. I found one on super clearance for $3.98 a yard. At that price, my fabric would cost $59.70 plus shipping and handling. Not too shabby. Still, I decided to check to investigate a bit further.

Common Yardage Chart

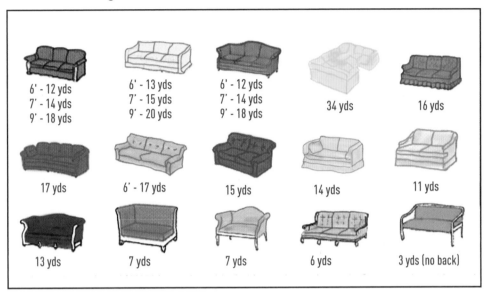

6' - 12 yds 7' - 14 yds 9' - 18 yds	6' - 13 yds 7' - 15 yds 9' - 20 yds	6' - 12 yds 7' - 14 yds 9' - 18 yds	34 yds	16 yds
17 yds	6' - 17 yds	15 yds	14 yds	11 yds
13 yds	7 yds	7 yds	6 yds	3 yds (no back)

Save by using a drop cloth

I went to Pinterest and searched for "Slipcovered Furniture" and found a great post on *Miss Mustard Seed*, a blog by Marian Parsons. She has lots of lovely examples of using a painter's drop cloth for slipcovers instead of purchasing fabric by the yard. I could purchase two large drop cloths (9x12) at my local hardware store for $15 a piece for a grand total of only $30! The painter's drop cloth is the right weight and the right price! Voila, the perfect fabric!

Preparing your drop cloth

I've got to admit I got a little carried away reading the comments online about how to prepare your drop cloth. I got lost in cyberspace with a million different opinions on how to do it correctly. It made me a wee bit nervous. But what I did worked, so I'm going to explain it step by step and hope you have as much luck as I did.

Hardware stores often have sales—look for coupons in your Sunday paper or those leaflets they send in the mail. I was able to get my drop cloths for 15 percent off, saving me an extra $4.50. Which is not much, I agree, but it could buy one delicious fudge brownie, which is worth its weight in gold.

First, I washed each drop cloth separately in my washing machine with hot water to shrink and soften them. Next, I filled my tiny four foot bathtub with enough hot water to submerge each cloth individually and swirled in four cups of bleach. Normally I wouldn't measure such a thing because I'm pretty haphazard with stuff like that, but because I had to bleach them separately I wanted to make sure the color turned out uniformly. I let the drop cloth soak overnight in the bathtub and swished it around several times. Because the drop cloth kept floating up, I placed large white plates and heavy bowls on top to keep the fabric completely submerged. I'd read online that some people were having problems with splotchiness, so maybe this technique is key to reducing uneven color. Worked for me.

Finally, I took the drop cloth out of the tub and washed it in the washing machine with hot water again, this time with fabric softener. I dried it on high with five or six fabric sheets. The result was a lovely soft white that was durable, yet soft to the touch. The color was not a stark white as you might imagine—it was more like a cream or very light oatmeal. The drop cloth has a bit of bumpy texture—it's not perfectly smooth like brushed canvas—and this gives it a tiny bit of color variation.

Dye your drop cloth

Because my daughter already had lots of color in her curtains, bedspread, and rugs I decided to keep the couch neutral and go with the sandy white of the bleached drop cloths. But you could easily dye the drop cloths any color you like using Rit dye. Check out the custom color cart on the Rit website to make any color you like. Pretty cool, right?

Make a pattern on your drop cloth

If you like the idea of a drop cloth for the price and durability but really love bold patterns, consider using a stencil. You can purchase a stencil pattern online. I was tempted, but it added to the expense and time factor, so I decide to leave mine white, although I hope to try the stencil idea on another piece in the future.

SLIPCOVER: TIME VERSUS MONEY

If you have more time than money, learning to upholster the piece yourself on a free piece of quality furniture is the way to go. If you don't have much time and a small budget, you might choose to buy and dye a drop cloth like I did and have the cover made professionally. If you have mounds of cash, you might decide to buy a new piece and leave it as is, or customize it by changing the fabric.

MORE DIY MONEY SAVINGS TIPS
Continued ...

Frame things other than expensive art

I love art and I would encourage you to support your local artists big time, but if you are on money crunch there are a few ways to give your walls some lovin' without breaking the bank. Besides framing photography,

I fell in love with this printed paper that I found at Essentials, a wonderful design-focused paper shop in Northampton, Massachusetts. The frame came from a thrift store for ten dollars.

which is usually a pretty affordable route, you can also think about hanging children's art, framing a lovely wallpaper, or even a favorite fabric. The nice thing about framing items that aren't super expensive is that you don't feel bad about changing them once in awhile. Lots of stylists will tell you to change such accessories as pillows and curtains for the season, but it's also nice to freshen up your space by changing the art around, whether it's moving it to a new location in your home or slipping something new in a frame.

Make your own curtains

If you can sew a straight line, you can make curtains. Isn't that cool? I think it's the best news ever. Does it mean I make all of my curtains? Heck *no*. But,

I have made a few. My favorite curtain hangs in my half bath downstairs. It's a café curtain, one that hangs halfway down, letting the light drift in from the top third of the window. I love this one so much because my artsy friend Hillary made me this amazing "hand towel" full of hand stitched goodness that was just too pretty to be used as a hand towel, but too small for a curtain. So, I went to my local super sweet fabric store, Delectable Mountain, and bought some lovely thin blue and white fabric. I sewed the tea towel onto that. Then, I made a seam of about an inch, long enough for a curtain rod, and *boom* it was done. The curtain rod was

Handmade design stitched by artist Hillary Duggan.

literally one of those squeeze jobs that cost a dollar or two at the hardware store and the pretty fabric was less than ten bucks. But let's be realistic, it's mostly nice because my dear friend poured her love into hand stitching the original design. I think of her every time I see it, which is kind of funny because it is in the bathroom. But still, that's nice, right?

Vintage fabric makes for great bathroom curtains. Simply cut down the middle, sew a one-inch seam at the top and voila, a lovely little curtain.

That same nice friend also gave me a yard of really pretty vintage fabric. I cut it right down the middle, sewed the same style one-inch seam, added the same squeezy cheap curtain rod and another café style curtain is born in my full bath and I love it, too.

Don't have any nice friends to make you cute hand stitched tea towels or give you vintage fabrics? You really should get on that. But truly, there are so many cute tea towels out there. Some of my favorite ones are sold at Anthropologie. I usually can't fork out a couple of hundred dollars for a dress, but I surely can round up $12.50, which is the price of their sweet little tea towels. You can easily make curtains out of them. Or how about stitching together some fabrics you already have in the house? Scarves? Your favorite old tee shirt? There are endless ways to use what you've got and make some original rad curtains. You got this one, girl.

Think Outside the Box: Part 1
How to Use your Home to Generate Income

If you could use an extra dolla' let me hear yah holla! Even if you are not on a tight budget, perhaps there are a few things you'd like to do to your space and you just need a little extra dinero to help you on your way. I'd like to suggest that you consider using your home to generate income.

In Chapter Two, we learned how Erin Gandy made a private rental space in her home which helped pay for grad school. Suzanne Kingsbury split her home into two apartments, so the rent she collects practically pays her mortgage. Susie Belleci and her husband received a $3,000 grant to help them construct a small, private studio apartment within their home in Vermont.

I've done it too. When we first moved into our home, there were so many things I wanted to do. I was working part time and had a one-year-old, so I didn't have a lot of extra time or money. Thus, we rented our extra bedroom to short-term guests—primarily grad school students from my alma mater and kids from the circus school just down the road. I liked renting to these guys because they were generally pretty laid back and fun. Plus, their schedules were such that they were often only here for a few months and rarely here in the summer or holidays, which meant the room was free to accommodate my friends and family when they came to visit.

Plus, renting for a few months at a time is handy because if you don't like the person they will be moving along shortly. But, in fact, we had very good luck with renters and enjoyed getting to know these crazy characters. Now that hubby and I are both working, we don't need to rent our guest room anymore, but that income alone helped us remodel both of our bathrooms and purchase needed supplies such as paint for DIY projects. Okay, I might have bought a couple of Anthropologie dresses along the way, too.

WAYS TO USE THE SPACE YOU HAVE TO GENERATE $$$

- Rent a room out of your home or apartment on a short-term basis to college students in your area.
- Rent a room out of your home or apartment over the weekend.
- Convert a space in your home into a private long-term rental space.
- Consider swapping homes when you go on vacation and save a bundle.
- Rent your home on VRBO while you are on vacation and earn cash.

Consider This . . .
Say you rented your guest room on the weekend for $50 a night on Airbnb. That's $100 per weekend. If you rented it twice a month, that's an extra $200 a month for you and you'd only have guests four nights a month (minus Airbnb fees). If you did this year round, you could earn up to $1200 or way more depending on your fees and how often you rent.

Online Resources to Help You Rent Your Space
Airbnb.com
VRBO.com (Vacation Rental By Owner)
HomeAway.com
Craigslist.org

Think Outside the Box: Part 2
How to Use Your Home to Save Big While Traveling

Do you love going on vacation as much as I do? I love to travel—the only problem is that I am a budget traveler with luxury taste! Solution: homeexchange.com. Here's how it works. You build a profile on the site and then say where you are interested in traveling and what dates you are available. Other home exchangers might contact you based on your profile, or you can be more proactive and search for homes you'd like to stay in and contact them directly. You can do simultaneous or non-simultaneous exchanges and there is a small monthly fee to join.

Here's how it's worked for me. Within weeks of joining homexchange.com I found an exchange for two weeks in San Miguel Allende, Mexico. So instead of being up to my elbows in snow, this February I'll be floating down cobble-stoned streets in my maxi dress shopping at the local market and I couldn't be more thrilled about it.

The lady who I am exchanging with is no fool. She asked for a non-simultaneous exchange and she'll be coming to my Vermont home in July when the weather is mild, the rivers are flowing, and the gardens are in full orgasmic bloom. Where will I be in July? On book tour, my dear!

Online Resources for Home Exchange

HomeExchange.com

LoveHomeSwap.com

Intervac.com

Craigslist.org

GuestToGuest.com

chapter 9

DECISION MAKING 101

First, some background. My oven blew out about three months ago, so obviously we needed a new one. But I'd been searching for the perfect chandelier for ages. When you're on a budget, how does one choose? Do you go for the practical oven or the glistening chandelier?

This is not the first time I've been challenged with this practical versus whimsical sort of decision-making dilemma. Should I leave my very stable and respected job in academia, or quit and stay home to write a book on personal development and home décor? Should I keep my child in school like the rest of the civil mothers, or whisk her off for a month (or year!) to some exotic foreign country to be immersed in another culture and language?

It seems I have an innate genetic coding that steers me toward the wild side. At age three I asked myself whether I should wait patiently for my family to get in the freakin' car, or teach them a lesson and take charge behind the wheel. It was pretty exhilarating watching my entire extended family running down the street in their Sunday best.

When I was twelve I had a key made to my mother's car while she took a nap. Was this a good decision? Not so much, but it did get me to the mall when I skipped school. Sorry, Mom.

And today, I took the day off and drove an hour and a half to New Haven, Connecticut, to spend some quality time with my friend, Anthropologie. It's okay, my boss knows (why do you think they make such things as personal days? To go to the Dentist? Don't be silly.)

Now, don't get me wrong, I can be practical. I get my daughter and myself to work and school daily. I pay the mortgage, cook dinner (sometimes), and do lots of other practical things, like buy a Subaru instead of a convertible (though I did get the one with a giant sunroof).

But sometimes a girl just needs to have some fun, no? And thus, one lovely Vermont evening I sat drinking mojitos with my best friend, Ayda. In a tipsy flurry I showed her all the things I had on my dream list for my home, and then went on to cry about how I had to spend $500 on a stupid stove instead of the glorious chandelier that I was coveting. As I stumbled to show her the beauty online, I was astounded to discover it was on *sale*! And shipping was free!

Ayda shouted, "*Buy it*!!!"

Still, I recall a little inner voice (probably that of my mother) saying, "Are you really going to buy a chandelier instead of a stove?"

About two months later I happened to look out my window to check out the snowdrift, and what was this on my front porch? A giant box? I rushed out, ripped it opened, and discovered my surprise . . . a gorgeous, sparkling chandelier. I must have had one too many mojitos that night . . . or maybe exactly the right number. Smile.

Was it practical to buy a sparkling chandelier rather than the stove? You'd be surprised what a toaster oven can do, my friend.

THINK ABOUT IT QUIZ:
How practical are you when it comes to home décor? Are you more influenced by others or by your own intuition? Take this quiz and find out.

1. Your husband *hates* the idea of wallpaper, but you know it's in. What do you do?
    A. You buy it anyway, he'll grow to love it.
    B. You hire someone to do it and tell your hubby it was an accident.
    C. You obey "the man" and do as you are told.

2. Your heating system is over thirty years old and you've been told it needs to be replaced in the next year or two. It will cost $8–10,000. But, you've also been talking to a contractor about updating your kitchen. It's the room where you and your family spend the most time, but it's the smallest and most awkward room in your home. Estimated costs are $10,000. You can't do both at the same time. Which do you choose?

    A. You were once told you needed a new motor, but you drove the car for five more years. You'll deal with the heating system when, *or if,* it really needs replacing. You go for the kitchen remodel without hesitation.

    B. Nervous about not having heat, you take out an extra home loan but continue with the kitchen remodel—hey, both items will help with the resale value, right?

    C. The idea of more debt makes you cringe and heat is essential. The kitchen will have to wait.

3. You've been searching for the perfect couch for months and although you are on a budget, you accidently found *the* one, but it's double the price you'd hoped to pay . . .

    A. This is a once in a lifetime opportunity! Something else will have to give. The perfect couch does not come along every day.

    B. You want this couch, but not as bad as you want to stick to your budget. You ask about payment options and start thinking about how much you could get for your old couch on Craigslist.

    C. Are you kidding? That's two months of groceries.

4. There's an extra room in your house, so you . . .

    A. Think about adding a bar, or art room, or maybe an *art room with a bar?*

    B. Take a poll asking each member of your family how they would like to utilize the room.

    C. Turn it into a guest room. After all, your mother-in-law is coming to visit in five months.

How'd Yall Do?
If you answered mostly with As:

You are wild and go for your desires no matter the costs. I admire the fact that you know what you want. Keep that spunk, but find a way to let your loved ones know they matter, too. Don't worry, you will still get your way, my dear, but let them think they got theirs, too.

If you answered mostly with Bs:

You don't like to rock the boat, do you? You are good at compromising, but at what cost? Be careful that you don't give up too much of what's important to you to please the status quo.

If you answered mostly with Cs:

You do the "right thing" all the time. Honey child, life is short. Please loosen up and break a rule or two!

chapter 10

A ROOM OF ONE'S OWN, HOW TO CREATE YOUR SWEET SPOT HOME ONE ROOM AT A TIME. FEATURING *DESHA'S CABIN.*

I was talking with a friend the other day about how we want our homes to be beautiful all the time, and that the reality is that we are both working mothers who also have tons of creative projects and sometimes things just get messy! She reminded me of a little succulent plant that I had given her as party gift for one of my events, and how most of her plants had died due to lack of attention, but this little succulent sat in a dainty china tea cup on her window sill atop a linen tea towel in her kitchen, so that when she was washing dishes she was calmed by its simple beauty. This story reminded me of the importance of having at least one space in the home that is perfectly beautiful, even if it's just one little windowsill.

I have a space like this. I call it my *Cabin*. It's the place I go to have a cup of tea and read a magazine or light candles with my husband and have a glass of wine once our daughter is asleep. It's a tiny room in between my garage and my back porch and it's just perfect! But, it wasn't always that way. Oh no, in fact it sat for five years full of cobwebs, patio furniture, and—dare I say—a big ugly black grill. Heaven forbid!

The day we first looked at this home, I thought to myself, "Ah, yes, this little room is a gem, perfect for a little studio, children's play spot, or mini greenhouse." It was part of the reason we bought the house, but somehow it was abandoned until one fine day I was hit by a strong desire to make it pretty. I had a hundred other things planned for that day, and I ignored them all.

I enlisted my five-year-old daughter's help and began removing all the junk, cobwebs, and five years worth of dust. Underneath appeared a lovely barn red wooden floor! I swept and mopped it on my hands and knees. The walls were covered in some kind of weird muck, so I scrubbed them clean, but it was clear they still needed some serious TLC.

I turned to my daughter for advice. "What color should we paint these sad walls?" Her response, "*Pink!*" Luckily, I had some very light pink paint in the basement left over from another project.

Later that very day, I happened to drive by a load of furniture sitting on the side of the road with a sign that read FREE. I picked up a lovely green velvet chair. I bought a little jute rug at another tag sale for $1. At the same tag sale, a man gifted my daughter with an antique painting of a horse (we love horses!).

Once we arrived back home, we put all our tag sale treasures into the *Cabin*. My daughter added things she loved including some seashells from our trip to Mexico, some lovely jade rocks, feathers and found stones. I added a few things I love such as framed family pictures, pottery, and my beloved decorating books.

In one day, we had transformed our dirty little storage area into a real gem. It reminded me of my husband's tiny little room he rented when we first met which we called "the cabin" and thus, we christened our new space the *Cabin*. The moral of this story is this—you don't need a ton of time, or money, to create a special spot in your home. What you *do* need is a bit of motivation, a little patience to find the right thing, and an open mind that it will turn out just perfectly when the time is right.

Are You Utilizing Your Space Well?

When thinking about the overall design of your home, are there any rooms that are being underutilized? For example, I have a fairly decent sized dining room that is located in between my living room and kitchen which contains a large dining table, chairs, and a low hutch that contains art supplies, fabrics, and such. The only time we really use the dining room is when a group comes over for dinner, or sometimes we use the table for art projects, but often the art projects end up on the floor in the kitchen. In fact, pretty much every thing we did ended up in the kitchen. When people come over, they go straight to the kitchen.

The problem is the kitchen is one of the smaller rooms in our home, with not a lot of seating or space. I started thinking about how the kitchen was over utilized while a big empty space set right next to it—totally underutilized.

The only thing stopping us from using that space was a wall. I really wanted to take down that wall and open up the kitchen to the dining room completely, but there were a few problems. One, it's the only wall we have in the kitchen that doesn't contain windows or doorways, which means there are limited places to put appliances and cabinets. Two, it's a load bearing wall, which means it holds the integrity of the home and we'd need to add a very big piece of wood to stabilize the wall lest it all fall down!

We decided to compromise and just make a pass-through with a bar on the dining room side. This would allow light to pass through directly from the dining room to the kitchen and we could direct visitors to sit at the bar and hang out while we cook on the other side.

And you know what? When we knocked the hole in the wall to create the pass-through, we discovered knob and tube wiring inside the wall, which is very expensive to remove and replace . . . we are talking thousands of dollars. That's when we were glad we had not tried to knock down the whole wall—whoosh!

We quickly patched the area with the knob and tube wiring, which meant we had a smaller hole/pass-through, but it still looks great and has changed the way we use the dining room and the kitchen. Instead of being underfoot when I cook, my daughter uses the dining room much more because we can see each other from the pass-through. She can sit right across from me at the bar and have a snack or make art while I wash dishes or prep for dinner.

Now that there is more light we eat all of our meals in the dining room instead of the smaller kitchen. My theory worked, and we are utilizing our space more efficiently. Yippee, smile, smile!

Is there a room in your house that is being over or under utilized? Let's THINK ABOUT IT. Check out the quiz on the next page.

THINK ABOUT IT QUIZ

Are you utilizing your space well?

1. Is there a space in your home that it being over-utilized? What are the problems that come with your over-utilized space? Is it too cramped? Too cluttered? Too many people wanting/needing to be there at the same time? How can you move some activity away from that space into another nearby space?

2. Is there a spot in your home that is under-utilized? What are you currently using the space for? Has it turned into a "junkroom"? Is there a better way to use this space?

3. What can you do to make your spaces more user friendly? Could one small change renew your space and make you want to use it more? Check the boxes that apply and then set a date on your calendar to work on your project.
   - o Declutter
   - o Organize distinct areas for certain tasks
   - o Add new organization system (think baskets, shelves, etc)
   - o Add new lighting to calm or energize the space
   - o Refresh with paint
   - o Add a new sink to allow more use in the bathroom or kitchen
   - o Create space by opening the wall, or adding a pass-through
   - o Close a space by adding a curtain or wall divider
   - o And . . . what other ideas come to mind?

chapter 11

MANIFEST YOUR DREAM HOME

Are you getting to the end of this book and thinking, "That's nice. I'm glad these Beetch-es have their dream homes . . . but I am a single mom with two kids, or I'm in debt beyond belief, or I'm too young, or I'm too old, or I'm too whatever to make this happen in my life."

In a big way I've written this book for you, my friend. I didn't always have the home of my dreams. In fact, there were many obstacles and you might say I was lucky in the way my home came to me (or super unlucky some might also say!). But, if it's been pure luck that I am living in the home of my dreams, it's also pure luck that I am engaged in work I love, have friends that support and love me, an amazing daughter, the car I want, and an overall pretty damn

good life. So if it is *luck*, then I've created my luck. And so can you. I share the following story to those who doubt, in the hopes that you can have a little faith and allow yourself to dream, because there is power in the dream.

MY STORY

In 2005 I joined a lunch time group run by my BFF Craig Cullinane, a master manifester and dream facilitator. We met weekly during lunch at Amherst College and discussed our hopes and dreams. We started by reading the book *Overcoming Underearning* by Barbara Stanny. Now, I have to tell you that I'd been into personal growth and awareness for many years prior. I'd read numerous books on expanding your thoughts and money, I'd travelled abroad to build self-awareness and a worldy perspective, and I'd attended a liberal grad school that's all about self-awareness and growth. In fact, I felt I had a Master's in personal growth even before we started this group.

So in one way I felt I didn't need to read another book on this topic. I knew all there was to know. And while I was a good student of the New Thought movement, there was still a deep inner feeling of skepticism that went way back to when I was a little one.

BFF Craig Cullinane and Desha at a Lady Gaga concert in Boston.

Regardless, I loved my friend Craig and knew it would be fun. Plus it would allow me to escape my office job that I was beginning to loathe. So, I committed.

The first activity in the book was to make an intention. Mine was *abundance*. Before we got to chapter 3, I discovered I was pregnant!

Woah partner! My group jokingly called me a Master Manifester. It wasn't my intention to get pregnant when I said "abundance." I meant cold hard cash. That was my first lesson in being specific for naming my desires!

While I was overjoyed at becoming pregnant, I was also full of sorrow because it meant staying in the job I hated. We needed my insurance and income more than ever. All of a sudden, I felt trapped. Confined. Ick.

About that time, there was an exercise in the book that instructed us to state a clear intention of our deepest desire and this time I knew I needed to be super clear! I knew exactly what my deep desire was, but I refused to wish for it because I couldn't bear the disappointment of hoping for something that was clearly impossible. And besides, if I spent my time dreaming for something that was unrealistic, I would end up without a *plan*, and then I'd really be sorry.

Thus, I spent every waking moment on the *plan*. But, the plan wasn't a plan; it was just plain old worry.

My BFF (who is pretty darn amazing) said to me, "What if you let go of your worry for a little bit and focus on your desire?" Just try it for three months.

I was skeptical. I was scared of the disappointment. But I tried it. I wrote down my intention and read it day and night. This is what it said:

My Intention is to . . .

1. Quit my job.
2. Stay home with my child for the first year of her life.
3. Buy a lovely home.

Number three was a biggie. I grew up in a tiny duplex and dreamed of living in a beautiful historic home. More than anything, I wanted to give my baby that experience.

But let me share that money was tight. I'd just finished a master's degree. We were in debt with no savings and we needed two incomes. I think you can agree that the typical route to buying a home does not generally coincide with quitting your job, especially when you are pregnant and broke with no savings!

But I was persistent. I read my intention day and night. Three months turned into six. Six months turned into nine. And one fine day, my most amazing daughter was born.

A month passed.

I was on maternity leave. Soon, it would be time for me to go back to work. We didn't have an alternate plan. Worry set back in. While the doula watched our infant, my husband and I went for our first walk alone to talk about what to do

next. I remember saying, "I can*not* go back to work. We must figure out a way for me to stay home. What are we going to do???"

And then my life changed in an instant.

In that very moment, my neighbor's jolly dog came running up and somehow managed to trip me. I fell to the ground and broke my femur. It was serious. It was trauma. It was more than bad. I was in the hospital for a week without my newborn child. Morphine. Surgery. *Tears.*

But I got better.

And then I got much better when the dog's owner told me they had home owner's insurance and they wanted to use it to pay for all my expenses and for my pain, which ended up being enough money for me to . . .

1. Quit my job.
2. Stay home with my daughter until she was nearly three.
3. Buy a lovely home.

We moved in just in time to celebrate my daughter's first birthday.

6 TIPS TO MANIFESTING THE HOME OF YOUR DREAMS
(OR ANYTHING ELSE FOR THAT MATTER!)

1. Write a simple, clear intention and place it above your bed or somewhere that you can see it and read it day and night.

2. Write a page long description of your new home in the present tense giving details about the feel of the home and things that you love. For example, mine included a front porch, gardens, and cozy feel. Read this periodically.

3. When imagining your home try to stay positive and exude good feelings. If you start feeling like the activity is impossible or stupid, just set those thoughts aside. Allow yourself to dream in this state—you can pick up the worry later.

4. If you are totally freaked out by this, try manifesting something smaller first to build your faith. Perhaps you could shoot for $10 or an awesome dress. Then go from there.

5. Put action toward your dream. While envisioning my dream home was part of the process, I also started looking at real estate and learned the facts about interest rates, etc. I didn't have the money, but I acted like I would soon and needed to prepare. I also took a free six week class on home ownership and applied for a grant that allowed us to pay all the closing costs (a total of $6,000).

6. State your intention with a clear heart and mind. Never ask for anything that could hurt anyone or anything. Keep your intentions pure and in line with your higher purpose.

Cheers baby . . . to finding your own Sweet Spot Style!

You might say this is a mighty coincidence and you could be right. And trust me, I would never ask to break my femur in order to fund my life. In a way, I was sending mixed messages. I was fully acknowledging my desires when I read my intention. I wanted to have hope and faith, but at the same time I was skeptical and scared.

It's my hope and intention that my clothing, home, gardens, and lifestyle reflect who I am and evoke feelings of warmth, light, generosity, openness, kindness, beauty, creativity, originality, and comfort. I hope that *Create the Style You Crave on a Budget You Can Afford* evokes those feelings in you—maybe it will inspire you to notice what makes you feel good and surround yourself with those things—all the while discovering and creating your own delicious Sweet Spot.

I think the universe delivered my intention the only way it could, in a very unlikely, impossible scenario. Since then, I've honed my manifesting skills. I've paid more attention to the details. I've taken notes and expressed my gratitude. I've started groups and supported other women who are on the edge of their desires. I've tested the theory and it works. Beyond the house, I've manifested amazing jobs for myself and my husband, a new car, vacations abroad, and an overall Sweet Spot life. Of course, when I set my intentions now I always add "in a healthy and safe way for me and my family."

ONE LAST THINK ABOUT IT QUIZ

- Did this book inspire you?
- What did you learn?
- Are you creating a meaningful home environment that expresses your values and personal style?
- Are you transforming your home into your own private Sweet Spot?
- Have you used intention to conjure your dream home?

Now I'd like to hear your story. Please join me online and share your own *Sweet Spot Style* story at SweetSpotStyle.com

I'm Not Ready to Say Goodbye, Are You?

I'm not very good with goodbyes; I'd prefer a nice "see ya later." My intention with writing this book is to encourage you to think about how you are in control of your home environment, how you can choose to create it any way you want to allow you to feel the way you desire. I hope that through the shared stories you will feel inspired to create a space that uniquely reflects your values and what is important to you. You can rest assured that perfection is not the goal, but living in a way that suits you in this time and space is a good place to start. There is no right or wrong way to do it, no judgment here.

And beyond home décor, my wish is for you to take these lessons and use them in every part of your life, to consciously create your relationships, your career, and your life in a way that feels you are living fully in your Sweet Spot.

May you continue to create the life you crave!

Join me online at SweetSpotStyle.com for more resources on living in your Sweet Spot, including one-on-one consultations and group e-classes.

Thanks for reading!
xo Desha

About the Author, Photographers, and Contributor

DESHA PEACOCK

Local celebrity and award-winning TV show producer/host and lifestyle blogger, Desha Peacock is known for her eclectic style and helping others see the possibility within themselves and their homes. When she was just twelve years old, Desha turned to her mother and asked, "Why did I have to be born in such a boring place as Sherwood, Arkansas?"

Since then she's traveled to nearly every continent in the world. An avid seeker of beauty and culture, she's explored the bazaars of Africa, the Middle East, Europe, and Central America. She's slept in two-dollar hostels in Guatemala and boarded million dollar yachts in the Mediterranean. Her world travels, mixed with her Southern charm have inspired Desha's unique eclectic/vintage/bohemian style that she is so well known for. Desha holds a master's degree in Intercultural Service, Leadership, and Management from the School for International Training, is a certified Global Career Development Facilitator and has facilitated groups in London, Costa Rica, Mexico, Dubai, and Abu Dhabi.

In her private Sweet Spot Style practice and in her four years as Director of Career Development at Marlboro College, she has counseled hundreds of clients and has been quoted in the Huffington Post, YahooNews.com, Career Rookie, US News Money, and more.

Desha currently lives with her husband and daughter in Brattleboro, Vermont.

To learn more about creating your own Sweet Spot Style in your life and home go to SweetSpotStyle.com.

PHOTOGRAHPERS

ELLE JAMES

Elle James is a Vermont-based photographer who loves capturing beauty in things that are raw and unrefined. Known for her use of light and shadow, her photography evokes a feeling of whimsy and nostalgia, yet has strong attention to composition, detail and color. She loves photographing fashion, nature, home décor, and her children.

JANAE HARDY

Janae Hardy has a degree in photography and art history, but says she feels blessed to live in the digital age where she can continue to learn online. After fifteen years of photography, Janea's passion for photographing interiors and people gets stronger each year. Being a photographer is most definitely a dream job!

ARSHIA KHAN

Arshia Khan is the photographer for *Arkansas Life Magazine* and *Sync Magazine*. She strives to find beauty in the details many miss in life. She's often found standing in the middle of a driveway, blocking traffic while snapping a photo of cracks in the pavement.

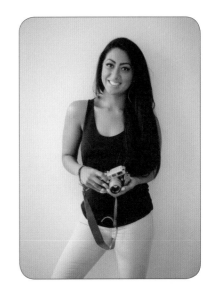

NANCY NEIL

Nancy Neil is a California-based photographer who's worked internationally for established designers such as Monique Lhuillier, Jerome C. Rousseau, Stewart+Brown, Petunia Picklebottom, etc. Her photography has been published in *Martha Stewart, Vogue, C Magazine, Architectural Digest* and many others. Nancy has a knack for capturing authentic, candid heartfelt memories in a casual, lighthearted manner. She lives in Santa Barbara on an eighty-acre ranch with her husband, two sons, and their trusty Australian Shepherd.

Thanks to the all of the homeowners who shared photos of their spaces and a special acknowledgment to the these talented professional photographers who submitted more than one story for this book. You ladies rock!!!

COLOR CONTRIBUTOR
Louise Gale

Louise Gale is a British artist, with a passion for color, pattern, nature and energy. She lives in Spain, overlooking the ocean with a distant view of Gibraltar rock, tiny fishing boats, and the North African coastline. Louise spends her days creating, running workshops and assisting other creative souls with their businesses. She spent eight years living just outside of New York City where she found the courage to leave her windowless corporate job and pursue a life filled with more creativity and freedom to find her own Sweet Spot in life. Her work has been published in the *New York Times* and featured in *Inc Magazine* as well as other publications. louisegale.com

Gratitude Brings Abundance

This book is dedicated to those who dare to live the life they crave. May all your dreams come true.

Remember in chapter 8 when I mentioned homeexchange.com and how I was dreaming of floating down the cobblestone streets of San Miguel de Allende, Mexico? Well, it's happening. As I sit in this beautiful light-filled café while my daughter decorates her handmade piñata in Spanish class, I can't think of a more perfect time to express my gratitude. In this moment, my heart is overflowing with joy. Two years ago, who would have thought that I would be spending a month in sunny Mexico, finishing this book, and giving my first international Sweet Spot Style workshop while having a grand adventure with my favor-

ite person in the world, my daughter? And yet, it wasn't luck that brought me here. I am an optimist and allow myself to dream, but I also depend *a lot* on other dreamers for support.

I would like to express my heart-felt gratitude to those who see the vision with me, encourage the dream, and who say yes with me. Those include master manifestor Craig Cullinane, supreme optimist Mary Shymanski, fun-loving Ayda Robana, vision encouragers Susie Belleci and Lizzie Rosenberg, and path-maker Susie Crowther.

For saying the words, "you should write a book on style" and then making it happen, agent Dede Cummings. For book design, editing, and all around support and unconditional patience, Abigail Gehring Lawrence. To artist and color contributor Louise Gale, mood board contributor Ashley Pahl, my darling photographers, and to all of the amazing folks who shared their stories and homes.

To Holly Becker of decor8, thank you for sharing your story and lighting the way for bloggers around the world.

Thank you.

For branding and dream and empire building, let me thank dear friend and business guru Suzanne Kingsbury. For creative mojo and love: Sarah Johnson, Corri Bristow, and Robin MacArthur. For the many hours of brainstorming and sharing your creative photographic magic, I am thankful for you, Elle James.

To my mother, who taught me to have faith and expect miracles, and to my brother with his never-ending encouragement, I am lucky. To hubby, who in my mother's words "has to live with all of my ideas and wild spirit." To my daughter, who nearly knocks me over when I receive good news, even when she doesn't quite understand the details.

And to all my Fire Starter Soul Sisters, keep manifesting your deepest desires.

desha peacock

• • • •

Photo Credits

Cover: Justina Blakeney

Abigail Gehring Lawrence: viii, x, 142, 143 (lower two), 184 (bottom), 216
Ashley Pahl: 162
Arsala Khan: 241 (top)
Arshia Khan: 100–115, 160
Daniel Kornguth: 68–73
Desha Peacock: v, 6 (upper right only), 8 (middle, lower left), 11, 24–30, 145, 147, 165, 168 (collage to the left), 175 (upper left, right), 178, 181, 182, 191, 201, 202, 226, 234
Elle James: 6 (except for upper right), 7, 8 (lower right), 12–19, 56–67, 122–137, 143 (top), 144, 167, 168 (right), 169, 170, 172–174, 175 (middle left), 176, 177, 184 (top left), 188, 194, 196–198, 199 (top left), 204, 207, 211, 212, 221–225, 229–234, 236, 239, 240 (top)
Iyla Neikirk: 243
Janae Hardy: vi, vii, 8 (top), 32-55, 183, 187, 190, 193
Justina Blakeney: 116–121
Katie Day: 240 (bottom)
Kelly Bone: 94–99
Leigh Aschoff: 241 (bottom)
Liz Karney: 186
Louise Gale: 155-159
Nancy Neil: 74–93, 148, 171, 175 (lower left corner)
Navyblur: 242
Per Nadén: 20-24
Rachael Rice: 138–141, 195
Sarah Johnson: 4
Shari Zarin: 200 (lower right)